THAT STRANGE LITTLE BROWN MAN GANDHI

THAT STRANGE LITTLE BROWN MAN GANDHI

FREDERICK B. FISHER

GYAN

Published by

Gyan Publishing House
5, Ansari Road
Daryaganj, New Delhi-110002
Phone: 011-47034999, 9811692060
E-mail: books@gyanbooks.com

Distribution Network
gyanbooks.com
India, USA, Canada, UK, Australia

ISBN: 978-93-7014-076-9 (HB)

First Published, 1932

2nd Impression 2025

Printed at: Gyan Press, Delhi.

THAT STRANGE LITTLE BROWN MAN GANDHI
Author: FREDERICK B. FISHER

Gandhi

© Keystone-Underwood

AT THE LONDON CONFERENCE

That Strange Little Brown Man

GANDHI

✡

BY

FREDERICK
B. FISHER

To

WELTHY HONSINGER FISHER

FOREWORD

I first met Gandhi in 1917. The Montagu-Chelmsford Reforms were then making ferment all over India; and Gandhi was just emerging into dominating national leadership. I conceived an immediate admiration for this amazing statesman of the new east, and that admiration has ripened through the years into friendship.

I last heard his voice over the trans-Atlantic telephone while he was in London this year at the India Round Table Conference. It was the same clear, vibrant voice. I could feel his warm personality across the three thousand miles of ocean and air. We talked for ten minutes about his health, his cause, the invitation to America, and his soul-call back to India. When he hung up the receiver he said, "I have been participating in a miracle," and then rushed off to a dinner with Lady Astor. He has been participating in a miracle for forty years—ever since his mature call to human service. His very life is a miracle to those of us who know him best.

India has been my home. Twenty-eight years ago I settled in Agra, the city of the Taj Mahal. Ever since then, I have gone back and forth between the east and west, and resided for a decade from 1920 to 1930 in Calcutta. I have had opportunity, therefore, to view each civilization, not only by familiar acquaintance, but through the necessary perspective of distance and comparison. In politics I am pro-Indian but not anti-British; in religion a Christian, but not anti-Hindu nor anti-Moslem.

In presenting Indian problems as related to the Mahatma's

life and work, I seek deliberately to view them through his eyes. Literature abounds giving the Anglo-Saxon bias, tone and argument. I try to turn us Anglo-Saxons around and reveal us to ourselves as the new, awakened, aggressive Indian patriots see us.

This book is a story of experience. An attempt to weigh eastern and western ideals, as well as spiritual weapons and machine guns, in the scales of practicability.

I use Mohandas Karamchand Gandhi as a telescope through which to view this balancing of forces because he is, without controversy, the outstanding personality of the new east. Without him, India, in fact the whole modern Orient, is like France without Napoleon, like America without Lincoln. I shall have failed in my purpose if I do not make you see behind the statesman, or politician, or ascetic, if you wish, Gandhi the man; the living, breathing, loving, serving, repenting, triumphant Gandhi, who is my friend.

CONTENTS

PAGE

Foreword vii

CHAPTER

I. A Statesman of Peace 1
II. Is He a Fanatic? 19
III. Indians in Africa 30
IV. The Fighting Pacifist 52
V. American Influences 72
VI. Can a Hindu Be a Christian? 85
VII. What's Wrong With Foreign Missions? . . 100
VIII. Sex in India 116
IX. Madame Gandhi 131
X. What Makes India Poor? 151
XI. The Spinning Wheel 167
XII. Hindu-Moslem Unity 179
XIII. Can India Rule Herself? 196
XIV. A Cooperative World 215

LIST OF ILLUSTRATIONS

At the London Conference . . . . *Frontispiece*

FACING PAGE

The Statesman at Work 26

The Young Barrister of London and South Africa . . 36

Gandhi and One of His Younger Enthusiasts 90

Madame Gandhi Shares His Sacrifice 144

Gandhi on Disarmament 194

He Makes Charlie Chaplin Laugh 208

Gandhi

CHAPTER I

A STATESMAN OF PEACE

"GANDHIJI! Gandhi the Beloved. Mahatma! The Great Soul of India!"

Like the sigh of a great wind this name swept over the white capped thousands as I rode on the train one day with Mohandas Karamchand Gandhi towards Calcutta. No word of his coming had been allowed over the government owned wires for fear of an uprising. Yet the curious grapevine telegraphy of India, ancient and mysterious, knows no censor. At every station I saw the human seas overflow our train. Ladders of breathing and sobbing bodies were made so that the lucky ones might climb to touch . . . or merely to see the Mahatma. Rose-petals covered our engine. Peasants stopped their bullocks in the fields and bowed in prayer as the holy train swept by. Every pole, fence, and hillock had its burden of worshippers. Why? Not for a little brown man spinning out his day of silence. The soul of India was worshipping not Gandhi, the man, nor merely Gandhi, the patriot, but Gandhi the Indian ideal . . . the hero who had turned moral force into a weapon, a weapon at once spiritual and political.

What a strange contradiction Gandhi is, then! In India a god: in England and America a cartoon. Newspaper pictures reveal him ugly, emaciated, toothless. The western world is bewildered at his power. We see in him a thin little brown man, walking on foot to the hundred million dollar palace of the Viceroy of India. We of the west look at this human god of the east, clutching his black umbrella, and say contemptuously, "Why, he is only a naked little man!"

Yet not so long ago this naked statesman came out of the Viceroy's palace with the fate of the British empire balanced in his bony fingers.

"What is his secret?" hundreds have asked me since I came home from twenty-eight years of contact with India. "He was your friend when he was plain Mr. Gandhi. Is he a saint or a fool? Is he a fanatic or a statesman? Does he for one moment dream that he can buck a machine-made civilization? That he can upset the world?"

That is exactly what Gandhi is doing . . . upsetting a world, a materialistic world, enthroned upon a preconceived right to rule by force of arms. He is succeeding not because he is a god, but because he is the man for the moment. There are many great leaders who never come to full authority or power because the time for their particular contribution to society is not yet come. The man may be right or the moment may be right: but it is only when the two conjoin that an hour of history is struck. Henry Ford would never have made his millions (which are valuable only as so much canned power) if he had been born fifty years sooner or later than he was. Gandhi epitomizes the post-war idealism. Yet he is preeminently practical, as our age is practical. This naked little Indian is even what the Scotch call canny . . . wise in the psychology of peoples. For he understands both the brown man and the white.

I remember one afternoon in Calcutta, during the session of the National Congress, how my hand reached out instinctively to grasp his in responsive emotion as he sat calmly addressing the great assembly in words of truth too big to be limited to one race.

I knew the genesis of this speech, for I had spent a week-end with him when we were both the guests of that regal host Rabindranath Tagore. Circumstances could scarcely have been more perfect for analyzing the contrasting personalities of these two giants. It is not easy to analyze the character of our friends. Gandhi has become a world-wide name; and Tagore is a fixed literary star of the first magnitude; I can only respond to an inner urge to reveal what I put in my note book during those days.

The time was September; the heavy monsoons were over; and the earth was bursting into fresh green life. It was easy in this tropical beauty to get up with the sun. I knew Gandhi's habits; so I ate my chhoti hazri (little breakfast) at sun-up. Knowing also the leisurely habits of Tagore, we did not venture into his drawing-room for conversation until mid-morning. The shade of his porch was welcome; it was more of a Roman porch than a room, open on all four sides; the bedrooms, kitchen, and the poet's study having a loose masonry connection with the four corners. Steps led down from each side into the fragrant garden. Beyond were mango groves, sal trees, and the old marble prayer bench that his father had used before him.

Gandhi was ready for conversation. He sleeps only a few hours, and his early morning meditations made him eager for active life. He and I walked up the terra-cotta steps, removed our shoes, and sat down cross legged just as our host entered in his ample flowing robes. His ideas were just as ample and just as flowing. We talked of gods and men, empires and democracies, poetry and history, east and west. Tagore led the way, steering clear of details and launching out into the wider paths.

Gandhi was silent for a long time. Charlie Andrews and I spoke very little. After a while Gandhi's passionate eyes began to gleam. We had come over into the realm of social injustices, politics, poverty, struggle. Tagore had seemed like a mountain. Gandhi leaped forth like a gushing cataract, pouring out his very life's blood as though upon an altar of his people. Every word was carefully chosen. Every gesture was deliberate. His body was well poised, but his eyes seemed like flashes of fire, and his lips were burning coals. Never did I see more clearly in any personality such absorbing love for men, and I have seldom heard more refreshingly scientific and practical suggestions for social improvement and growth. He had been planning his opening speech for the National Congress, and I knew it would be a great one. He crouched there against the wall, a picture of passionate patriotism, consumed by his spirit till his very body dwindled and left only—a soul—the soul of India.

SOWING FORCE

Down through thundering centuries the white man has been lord of the world harvest by conquest of arms. He did not invent conquest by force, but he developed this idea to such an exquisitely dangerous degree that with a few aerial chemicals he could wipe out all his enemies; but also himself. He has sown physical power and reaped gold and machines. He has planted not the cross, but the shadow of a cross, and has reaped an idealism too tenuous to bear the weight of passions unleashed, when nation snarls at nation. He has said to the brown and black man,

"I am the Great White Sahib. I rule you because it is for your own good . . . and because I want to."

But today the white man is not quite so sure of the pure profit in his harvest of force. If he has garnered glory he has reaped also chaos. Today his gold and machines lie alarmingly idle. Ten million white youths, and hundreds of thousands of black and brown, rot in the voiceless battlefields of his last war. He finds too late that he has planted armies and reaped a dark harvest of black death.

PLANTING IDEAS

But the white man has sown more than force of arms. He has planted ideas. Is he not a fit subject for Jovian laughter when he explodes into apoplexy to find the seeds of "equality", "self-determination", "freedom for all" which he has scattered to the four winds, germinating and blossoming in the dark east in a silent passion for freedom from white domination? This means, he suspects, force and more force if these seeds from his own garden, destined for his own consumption yet flown widely afield, are to be torn up or trampled down. What wonder if he is beginning to ask himself, "Isn't there, perhaps, some other way?" It is the hope of the western world that the thoughtful white man is beginning to suspect this force of arms, to sicken of the fruits of his own conquest.

A given state of society creates its opposite by carrying within its own womb the seeds from which children spring to slay the parent. This ironical economy of nature, bent on evolution, is as true today as it was in the days of Nero. It was the discovery of this law that gave Karl Marx that weird power with which he prophesied the proletarian revolt and the world crop of communistic dictatorships. The white man is beginning to realize that if he cannot control the perfected force of arms with which he has gained sway over five-sixths of the earth's populated surface, his very guns will turn on him and rend him. In gaining the world he is losing his soul.

It may at first glance seem startling that out of the supposedly backward nation of India should have come this championship of a new way of conquest: the heroic wielding of idealism as a sword . . . or more properly, as a machine gun. For there is nothing antiquated about Gandhi. He is as modern as each new morning and yet as old as time. And in this apparent anachronism lies his power.

Gandhi has taken the highest ideals of the Christian west, which we have not cared or dared to practise, and turned them against us in a new statesmanship of moral force, which is more powerful against us, doubtless, because it is forged from our own yearnings. His power is that in the one nation most fitted for his kind of religious and political experiment, at the exact instant when a war-torn chaotic world was thirsty for a new way of life . . . at this psychological place and moment, he has made our visionary ideal practical and has hitched it to his cart. For he believes that love, indeed, shall rule the world. What is more he has proved that, at least for a time, moral force can defeat machine guns.

That love can conquer the world is no new idea . . . it is as old as Buddha. But up to now it has been a moral conquest through the force of the spirit; a victory that had little to do with organized earthly power. When Jesus promised that the meek should inherit the earth, he did not mean that they should all become millionaires and kings.

Yet Gandhi is using the force of moral resistance as a political and an economic weapon, proving the power of directed spiritual force as practically potent to win battles against navies and armies. He is not a peace fanatic fed only upon goat's milk and impossible ideals. In the negative sense of the word he is not a pacifist at all . . . he is a fighter; but a fighter who will not shed blood. He knew war before he knew peace. For forty years he backed the mailed arm of the British Empire. He was a stretcher bearer in the Boer War in Africa. He was at the front during the "Zulu rebellion"; (the quotation marks are his, for how he asks, can a country rebel when the land is theirs by right of birth?) He recruited Indian troops for England during the World War which he, like many a westerner, was deluded into believing to be a war to end war. He is no brown faced, white livered ascetic. He has turned from a war of steel because he thinks it is no longer practical, and because he has seen enough of the scattering of men's bowels in the trenches of modern murder. Here is a man who is not afraid to face down his mistake.

"Confession of errors," says Gandhi, "is like a broom which sweeps away the dirt and leaves the surface brighter and cleaner. I feel stronger for confession."

Is it any wonder that the old school of international diplomacy finds itself dumb before a man as simple as that?

Whether Gandhi wins or loses immediate political freedom for his people, whether he rises to great power or is crushed in the maw of materialism is not the only vitally important issue in his bold campaign. India will achieve political autonomy eventually, whether it be by sword or passive resistance. Gandhi is more than a national Indian patriot: he is the personification of a new era.

"Civilization" says Gandhi, "is the conquest of one's mind and passions. We can conquer our enemy without hating him. Moral force is not idealistically but actually greater than navies."

This is a new idea in international statesmanship.

In each new epoch there is always a man who personifies the peculiar spirit of the age. Usually he is the fruit of seeds planted generations previously in the national life, waiting for the proper crisis to provide the climate for full fruition. Sometimes a whole continent is set aside to work out new ideals of civilization as North America, hemmed in by her sunrise and sunset seas, awaited the sowing of the seeds of political and religious freedom and the flowering of the lusty plant of representative democracy. So the Indian nation has patiently waited its day of blossoming.

BROWN ARYANS

Ancient India planted *Ahimsa* (non-violence) and reaped . . . Gandhi. He was born in spirit six thousand years ago when the history of the Aryan race began. Many people do not know that the majority of the present Indians, though burned brown by ten thousand suns, are Aryans of the same stock as the Anglo-Saxons. The traditional outcastes in India, the former Dravidians, were negroid in origin. The fact that intermarriage has been largely prevented by the caste system has kept these brown Aryans singularly pure in stock.

Gandhi got his practical understanding of *Ahimsa* from his mother. His parents were Jains, the Puritans of Hinduism, who held strongly to this particular doctrine of harmlessness.

I can still feel the silent awe with which I listened to his boyhood story of a deadly scorpion that ran across the floor of the living-room where his mother was teaching the children their Hindu Sunday School lesson, so to speak. His mother's feet were bare, with red painted soles. She followed the interesting Hindu custom of rouging them each morning after early devotions, in order to carry with her at her daily tasks, the pleasant odor and beauty of her prayers. As young Mohandas saw the deadly scorpion running straight towards those beautiful painted feet, he cried out in alarm,

"Mother! A scorpion! It will bite you! Kill it!" His mother said quietly,

"Be still, my son. If you do not frighten it, I shall not be hurt."

She watched the insect crawl up upon her heel, and then

slowly disengaging the silk scarf from about her shoulders, she reached down, picked up the scorpion, and dropped it out the window.

"Now it will neither harm me, nor I it," she remarked gently.

Lessons like this, coming from no printed page, but from the book of life, influenced the future life of a discerning boy. This gentle Puritan mother was one of the biggest factors in making Gandhi what he is today, a prophet of self-mastery, of national control through control of self. Over and over again he has said to his people that a nation whose citizens have not learned self-control, cannot rule itself as a national entity. This is a startling political theory. Upon that basis which of the white nations in either Europe or America is fitted for full self-government?

Gandhi's attitude towards the west partakes of the same attitude his mother had towards the scorpion. He knows the white world would bite, if he struck at it. Therein lies his astute, practical statesmanship. He does not try to use violence. That, we could understand and cope with. He uses a silk scarf against us . . . gentle ruthlessness against a sword. He drops us, figuratively speaking, out of the window, by refusing to cooperate with white rulers; and says to the English, and through them to the western world:

"Go your own way. Live your own life . . . but we Indians don't want you endangering our living-room. I don't want to kill you. Don't you kill me. But if you must kill me, I will be true, even in death, to what I believe."

Or, as his lawyer training fits him to do, Gandhi might in a flash turn this incident around and say in his gentle but pointed sarcasm to a nearby Englishman,

"If you would be happier to have us Indians play the part of the scorpion in the story, imagining yourself the mother nation, then develop poise and wisdom enough not to strike us in fear before we strike you. Just get up deliberately and shake us out of the window! That's all we want, our freedom!"

Then he would give his little chuckling laugh which I always love to hear, and say gently, "But after all, nobody's a scorpion. You're not. We're not."

It is partly this human ability to put himself in the other man's place and see his virtues as well as his vices, to see behind the aggressive Englishman and the erring Indian the true ideal for which each stands, that gives Gandhi his power as a statesman. His mind is not set in one permanent mold; it is fluid, ready to run into new channels as they open up. He has the adaptable power of the opportunist so necessary to successful statesmanship; he has the vision to forge harmlessness into passive resistance, the one anchor by which he could hold India. It was this same quality that gave him the shrewdness to recognize that in the innate idealism of the English race he had one of his greatest weapons for obtaining Indian freedom. He held a two-edged sword, and wielded it effectively.

Gandhi was educated in England. He studied law in London. He knows the Englishman at heart is decent, however imperialistic may be his policy as a state; that he as an individual does not relish shooting down any humans in cold blood whether they are white or brown. The march of world opinion since 1919 has moved towards peaceful methods of settling disputes. Perhaps not much progress has been made at European Round Tables. But a vast number of the people of the world crave understanding and peace.

Gandhi knows this. He is no demagogue, waving his people on to a slaughter in which they cannot win. He is a statesman, choosing the approved weapons nearest his hand . . . the only weapons for unarmed India . . . civil disobedience and passive resistance.

Gandhi is a practical general, cautiously directing the firing of his spiritual machine-guns of India. He has made the three policies of (1) passive resistance, (2) economic boycott, and (3) loving your enemies while hating the untruth for which they stand, formidable weapons. He comes from the *Bania* caste which is made up of tradesmen, money lenders and landlords, shrewdly concerned with pounds and profits. He belongs to the third generation of a family trained in the statecraft of the east which is not so different from European diplomacy as some would have us believe. He was trained both in India and in London to be a lawyer.

A FAMILY OF STATESMEN

The grandfather and two uncles of Mohandas Gandhi were successively prime ministers in the native State of Porbandar in Western India. It was in Porbandar that Mohandas was born, on October 2, 1869, and before he was eight years old, his father Kaba Gandhi was called to the court at Rajkot, a nearby native State, where he served as chancellor of the Exchequer. Kaba Gandhi was connected with this court until he died, so that Mohandas all through his school days heard the language of diplomacy and management of affairs as a part of his daily life. Indeed, he was schooled with the idea of carrying on his father's profession. But who could dream that instead of managing the business transactions of a small native state, as his forefathers had done, he would some day hold in his hand the political fortunes of three hundred and fifty million Indians!

It is perhaps significant that Gandhi speaks English with a slightly Irish accent! To further his father's plan of making Mohandas of value to his native state, the boy was early taught

English, and his first teacher was Irish. Perhaps the boy imbibed a taste for freedom along with his declensions. At any rate it was a new kind of Irish rebellion that he discovered; for instead of putting in Gandhi's copy-book the usual pap for young minds, "The dog ran after the cat", "Can you see the book?", the Irish educator had the young Indian copy, sentence by sentence, the Sermon on the Mount, and other great principles of life! The boy's slate-pencil scratched out daily,

> "Blessed are the peacemakers: for they shall be called the children of God."
>
> "Blessed are the pure in heart: for they shall see God."

First *Ahimsa,* do not kill any living thing for your own benefit; then the Sermon on the Mount. The education of the first world statesman with a practical plan of peace was coming on. Later he was to rediscover the Sermon on the Mount in its full beauty; but here in his early boyhood were planted the seeds that, watered by time and adversity, were later to flower into passive resistance and the aggressive moral standards of his full maturity.

Even in these early Indian school days, this small brown boy was an individualist, ready to experiment and decide things for himself. He not only smoked cigarettes when he could get them like any small boy in Kokomo, Indiana, but he also tried eating meat, one of the most terrible sins he could commit according to the Jain religion of his mother. The meat made him deathly sick, and combined with a guilty conscience produced terrible nightmares. So he went back to his regular diet with a sigh of satisfied relief.

Later on he was put out of his caste for breaking its rule

against going across the "Black Water" to England. Arrived in England he tried out being a young English dandy, donning a discreet morning coat, gray spats, and a walking stick. He even went in for violin and dancing lessons. But all of these foreign trappings brought him only self disdain and he promptly discarded them to bury himself in the study of law for which he had come abroad.

Most of Gandhi's critics fail to realize that he came to his loin cloth by slow and studied stages. He tried out western civilization and found it for the most part wanting. He had not yet robed himself in the principle of *Swadeshi,* home industries for India; but he was certainly giving the west a chance to show him, both superficially and actually what it had to offer. I repeat, he was an individualist. That he chose our Cross instead of our padded church pews, that he finally came to a loin cloth instead of a morning coat, does not necessarily prove him utterly lacking in constructive discernment.

It is a curious fact that here in London, after he had gone back to living on a few shillings a day and to cooking his own meals and studying instead of dancing, that Gandhi discovered the spiritual potency of the Sermon on the Mount, as well as the moral and literary beauties of his own Hindu Bhagavad-Gita (The Song of God).

A friendly Christian gave Gandhi a copy of the Bible while he was a law student, but the Indian yawned over Genesis and went to sleep over Exodus. It simply did not grip him. As he remarks naïvely, crystallizing the wails of the New England boy swamped in the "begats", "I disliked reading the book of Numbers." The Old Testament, that book of blood and thunder, of sons who cheated to obtain their inheritance and later became princes, of a "chosen people" brandishing a tribal god, had little to reveal to this disciple of *Ahimsa.* But the New Testament was a different thing. Here was a gospel he could understand. He ate it up. Here was meat he could devour.

> "But I say unto you, do not resist
> evil; whoever strikes you on one
> cheek, turn to him the other also."
>
> "And if any man takes away your coat,
> let him have your cloak also."

"That is the old Indian doctrine of harmlessness" said Gandhi. His childhood faith was confirmed by the highest authority of Christianity. At this same time he discovered similar passages in the Bhagavad Gita. It is strange that with such pious parents he had never read the Gita before. Perhaps it was best that the impact of the New Testament and of the Gita should strike him simultaneously and thus impress upon this coming statesman of peace the essential unity and idealism of all men and all religions. At any rate, it was in London with two Indian friends that Gandhi first read "The Song of God", and was at once struck by the fact that this supreme book of Hinduism supported and proclaimed some of the chief ideals of Christianity.

Gandhi's secular education proceeded hand in hand with his religious development. He passed his English law examinations with honor, and returned in triumphant enthusiasm to India with his diploma. When he was a student in London he had pictured himself as a prosperous barrister in the great city of Bombay; he would not stay in the small state as his father had done, but would go to the metropolis, and accordingly settled himself in Bombay. Here was a new variety of barrister; one who refused to prosecute for debt, and reserved the right to abandon a case which by his study he believed unjust. The first time he found himself standing to address the court, he became the old shy embarrassed boy of Porbandar; words left him, and in utter confusion, he sat down —a failure. That experience made him doubtful of his ability as a court lawyer, so he decided to try his skill at teaching. Finding his application was rejected, he returned to Rajkot, where he supported himself and his family by drafting legal papers. His brother was a man of considerable influence, and when a Hindu firm was looking about for a venturesome brilliant young lawyer who would go to South Africa and secure a claim for two hundred thousand dollars pending in one of the courts of Pretoria, he turned the offer in the direction of his younger brother and Mohandas accepted it at once. He set sail eagerly. His plan was to finish up this case within a year, and then return to India. But his practise grew phenomenally, and soon he found himself a rich young man. Within a few years his income was estimated to be about thirty thousand dollars a year.

Later the poverty and struggle of the African Indians cried out to him so loudly that he gave up all his wealth to the cause of freedom, and took a vow of poverty.

What other statesman with such power as Gandhi could muster only a spinning wheel, a clock, a cupboard, two filing cases, and $10 in cash, when the government came to confiscate his property because of patriotic refusal to pay taxes? Gandhi's power lies exactly here. He has proven that he could beat the material world at its own game: he could force business to yield to him wealth in amounts to cause envy even to western business men. Yet he saw in personal gain less profit than in service to his country. Just as he had seen in the system of war the seeds of its own destruction, so he beheld in private capital the destruction or subversion of spiritual values.

The moral life became as real to him as dollars, pounds and rupees. Does this prove him a fatuous dreamer? Far from it. Experiment is the approved method of this scientific age. Is a man any less practical, any less of a statesman, because he discovers in the slow laboratory of the years that gold and guns are not as powerful as moral force? War-torn and bankrupt Europe is painfully awaking to this same new revelation.

Perhaps also like Bernard Shaw, Gandhi recognized the ever newly discovered truth,

"This is the true joy in life, the being used for a purpose recognized by yourself as a mighty one; the being thoroughly worn out before you are thrown upon the scrapheap; the being a force of nature instead of a feverish little clod of ailments and grievances, complaining that the world will not devote itself to making you happy."[1]

NON-VIOLENT POWER

There was one more step to be taken in the building up of the new statesmanship which Gandhi was to develop as the peaceful warfare of the east. He had already the ideal of the power of concerted good-will. But this method, *Ahimsa,* was a negative virtue. He needed power and shells to shoot from his guns of the spirit. He must have a positive, aggressive force if he expected to win out against the force of arms. He found this in the principle of *Satyagraha.*

"Sat" is the Indian word for truth and *"Agraha"* means force. Truth-force was then the new word adopted for the principle of aggressive moral welfare which Gandhi conducted in South Africa just after the Boer war. He had no intention of becoming a reformer; it was forced upon him.

---

[1] Quoted by Haridas T. Muzumdar, *Gandhi the Apostle.* (Chicago, 1932.)

He had actually engaged his passage back home to India and was within a half hour of embarking when some of his compatriots asked him to stay over to assist them in their fight for recognition as human beings, even though they bore the blight of color which sets the ruled apart from the rulers of the modern east. Gandhi agreed to stay over until the next boat sailed; he stayed twenty years.

It was in Africa then that Gandhi first forged the weapon of truth-force with which two decades later he was to arm the millions of India against an imperialistic army bearing guns. "Passive resistance" is scarcely an adequate phrase with which to translate the combined force of *Ahimsa* and *Satyagraha.* In the pledge taken by the *Satyagrahi,* as the followers of Gandhi are called, occur the words, "We will faithfully follow truth and refrain from violence to life, person, or property."

But Gandhi adds a dynamic sentence,—"Non-violence does not mean meek submission to the will of the evil-doer, but the putting of one's whole soul against the will of the tyrant."

Gandhi also admits that in the nature of the two opposing forces, unarmed and unyielding resistance against machine guns, there will be a shedding of blood. But it is the blood of the Indians themselves which will be voluntarily shed, not that of the opposing forces. To thus put the force of self-sacrifice for truth, silently, relentlessly against arms till the very user of bayonets sickens of blood, is not passive weakness . . . it is militant courage of the highest type.

In using this method Gandhi is more than an idealist sending his obedient millions to the stake. (A stake he would willingly go to himself, if necessary, as all India knows. But the British will never knowingly allow this, for fear that with Gandhi gone such a wave of violence would sweep over India as would redden the very sea with blood.) Yet Gandhi, with all his ideals, is an astute statesman. Recollect that there are three hundred and fifty million Indians! that they have increased in population at the rate of thirty million during the past ten years. These millions, though unarmed, are trained to endure almost unbelievable hardships of poverty and famine. Millions of them have never had enough to eat. They are by nature soldiers of endurance.

What other warfare than that of Gandhi's could such a people carry on with any shadow of success? Can English machine guns slaughter three hundred and fifty millions without the world rising in protest? Gandhi may not win complete freedom for India all at once, but he is using the most potent and practical methods ever known to bring an unarmed nation to victory.

It is one of the greatest blunders of history that England failed to keep Gandhi loyal to the empire. Up to the time of the Amritsar rebellion and the Rowlatt Act Gandhi did his best to keep his people to the goal of self-government within the empire. He believed that individual Englishmen had made mistakes but that there was freedom ahead even for India, as for Canada and Australia, under the Union Jack. The British government in India could have had the leadership of Gandhi for a great, conciliatory, gradually developing program of Indian progress toward freedom. Instead they chose the way of armed repression, thus sowing the seeds of their ultimate defeat . . . for this blunder must ultimately cost them an empire.

CHAPTER II

IS HE A FANATIC?

DURING the World War when Indian soldiers voluntarily went to the front for England, when millions of gold flowed across the seas to buy ammunition for British guns, when self-determination for all peoples was in the very air, Gandhi with the rest of India, believed the British promise that after the tumult ceased India would have an autonomous government. It was the small matter of time upon which the final misunderstanding rested. India meant to have self-determination by rapidly advancing stages. England wiping her bloody brow said, "No thank you! We have already lost enough in this war. We do not intend to give you or your gold freedom now. In good and proper time, when, if ever, you prove your fitness to rule, we may make you a partly autonomous province."

But how can a nation prove its fitness to rule when it has no chance to practise ruling? Did America wait till her thirteen States were unanimous in intent and action before demanding liberty?

While Gandhi, student of history, was pondering this question, England instead of giving India the promised gradual freedom, clamped down upon her the Rowlatt Act. This was really a military provision giving the authorities powers superseding those of the civil courts. An Indian accused of having a revolutionary document in his possession could be court-martialed without benefit of trial by jury and without any right of appeal to a higher tribunal. As the crowning glory of the historically celebrated British constitutional justice, the accused was not considered innocent until proved guilty, as in all civil courts, but was held guilty unless he could prove the opposite!

Small wonder that when such bills were proposed Gandhi, as well as other Indian leaders, signed the historic protest declaring such laws "subversive of the principles of liberty and justice, and destructive of the elementary rights of individuals on which the safety of the community as a whole and the State itself is based." The Indians also affirmed that in the event these bills were passed, "we shall refuse civilly to obey these laws . . . but in this struggle we will faithfully follow truth and refrain from violence to life, person, or property."

Thus did passive resistance raise its head in India. April 6, 1919, was observed as a day of national humiliation. Gandhi, fearing violence, and afire with his principles of peaceful resistance, was here, there and everywhere, exhorting the people to patient warfare.

"I hope the speeches on April 6, will be free from anger or unworthy passion," he said. "The cause is too great and sacred to be damaged by an exhibition of passion. We have no right to cry out against suffering self-invited."

He was still determined to hate no man. He continued hopeful that the government would be brought by peaceful means to reasonable justice, and that self government for India, within the empire, could yet be attained.

THE AMRITSAR TRAGEDY

One of the places where both Gandhi and the government feared violent uprising was in the Punjab. The Punjabis are notoriously not a people given to lying down and being walked over without remonstrance. Amritsar in the Punjab is the religious capital of the Sikhs. Here is the beautiful Golden Temple, built like a floating castle in the middle of a lake. Here on the altar rests the sacred book of the Sikhs, worshipped by the reverent thousands that come long distances as devoted pilgrims. The early spring time of 1919 was the season for the people to flock in from the country to the temple to bring their offerings of flowers. Gandhi wanted to seize this opportunity to go to the Punjab and impress upon them his policy of non-resistance. The British officials would not permit him to enter the province. They made the further mistake of clapping him into prison. Moreover, the authorities jailed two of the leaders of the passive resistance movement in Amritsar. This was as fire to tinder.

In spite of official precautions, the government remained as uneasy as a woman afraid to look under the bed at night. Yet still the crowds made no move except to gather quietly to discuss the situation. Finally one day a small delegation went to the deputy commissioner to ask for the release of the two local leaders. Armed troops barred their way, who, when the crowd refused to disperse, fired upon the unarmed and innocent people. Maddened by the sight of their killed and wounded, the Amritsar Indians cut the telegraph wires and attacked two railway stations. Violence broke out, in sympathy, all over the Punjab . . . and Gandhi was not there to quiet it. The government had safely slammed into jail the only man who could have quieted the rising tide of anger of a persecuted people. Not that Gandhi resented the muzzling of the Indian people any less than did the Punjabis. He simply knew that to meet violence with violence was not the right answer.

Cannot a powerful government sometimes be the most childishly silly thing in the world? Nobody really knows how to use power anyhow. And the more thoroughly a government is organized the worse it is for a people when its officials become fear-stricken. Like a mad giant, cornered by perfectly obvious circumstances, it ignores reason and strikes violently in all directions. It is then a thing without mind or sense of humane direction. Brute muscles alone are in control. An individual may see and correct his fault, but mass emotions control a group.

The flocking of the religious pilgrims to Amritsar for the annual ceremonies was interpreted by the nervous government as a larger uprising. General Dyer, the military leader in command, sent out a ruling that not more than four people might congregate upon the streets at once. This official notice was made upon the street corners with drum beats, but the thousands of Indians flocking in from the country never heard of the ordinance at all. They simply went about their business. Since the crowds were there it seemed to Indian leaders a good time to hold a meeting at Jallianwalla Bagh, a walled garden, or small park, within the city, to discuss the present situation. Among other things the program called for "a denunciation of mob excesses" in accordance with the "nonresistance policy."

"At 12.40 he (General Dyer) heard that the meeting at Jallianwalla Bagh was to be held that evening. He took no steps to prevent it," says B. G. Horniman, a British authority who was in India as editor of a newspaper at the time of the Amritsar atrocity. "General Dyer waited for it to assemble and then he marched down on it with his force of rifles and machines. The thousands of helpless, unarmed people, some of them boys and children, were at his mercy, practically penned up in an enclosure from which they could only escape over walls, or through the entrances commanded by his soldiers. And deliberately, in cold blood, calmly directing the fire where the crowd was the thickest, he fired upon them for ten minutes until his ammunition was exhausted."[1]

With this governmental orgy of blood, a reign of terror began. Terror on the part of the whites trying to justify murder with more violence, terror for the Indians of whom five hundred had been killed and fifteen hundred wounded within the garden of blood. Since Dyer had decreed that no Indians were to be allowed upon the streets for twenty-four hours, the relatives of the wounded could not even give them a drink of water—and the English nurses were forbidden to attend them.

There developed a riot government, a government that had lost its head entirely. The administrators of martial law shut up suspected Indians in narrow cages for hours, where they were forced to face the burning sun. Gallows were erected upon the sidewalks to strike proper terror to the Punjabi heart. Indians were submitted to scorching humiliations, flogged naked, compelled to crawl on all fours along the sidewalks, to draw lines in the dust with their noses; lime-washed and exposed to the burning sun; children were flogged; and women forcibly unveiled and brutally outraged. Nero himself would have been hard pressed to think up any further atrocities. Yet so far was the government committed to the policy of the mailed arm that even though reports leaking through to England brought a protest of horror, the representatives of government commended General Dyer, and a public purse of one hundred thousand dollars was raised for him by indignant Toryites at home when the hiss of public opinion forced his recall from Indian duty.

What was Gandhi going to do now? The whole country turned its face toward the advocate of passive resistance.

---

[1] Horniman, B. G., *Amritsar and Our Duty to India.*

Could he see his countrymen washed in their own blood and still keep his belief in the policy of harmlessness and moral force? It is proof of his real statesmanship that this is exactly what Gandhi did. Even with Tagore and other Indian patriots cursing him he said,

"This is wrong. But hatred will not conquer wrong . . . only love can. I am a disciple of *Ahimsa.* It is enough. We will fight for freedom now. But we will not get it by killing one Englishman."

KILLING DOES NOT PAY

It was only Gandhi's statesmanlike poise and power, rooted in the deeply religious nature of the Indian people, that kept the Amritsar Congress which followed in 1920 from being the most violent thing in Indian history. Only his personal insistence that killing does not pay kept the people from a terrible massacre of revenge. Gandhi accomplished this end by setting up a constructive plan of his own for getting political freedom for India. He first inspired the angry people and then gave them something to do. These are the two primary laws of practical social psychology.

But how was he to build up his army of peace? There were three questions to be considered and settled. First,—he had taken his vow of *Satyagraha,* that is non-violent, non-resentful revolution against this violent governmental power. He could not therefore, organize an army of soldiers with guns nor call the people to violent action. Second,—the population of India was so dense and the people were so anchored to their own country that even though hundreds of thousands of men raised the cry that they ought to find some other territory and migrate there by millions, seeking some new land as had America, Gandhi's knowledge and common sense showed him that this kind of dream was wild and impracticable. He knew that these millions of people could not lift anchor and find homes elsewhere. What country could contain them? Thousands of Mohammedans did migrate to Afghanistan and other places, but they realized that white power even then was seeking sway there too. His third question was: How could the Indians remain in their own land and endure such suffering and loss of self-respect? Or how could they get freedom while remaining there without resorting to war and bloodshed? This was Gandhi's momentous question and this is where the greatness of the man revealed itself. It is this statesmanlike tackling of this complex problem that will give him rank in human history as one of the world's leaders.

He started by making a deep plea to the soul of India which believed fundamentally in the conquest of the spirit through suffering. For generations the holy men of India had endured agonies; beds of spikes, being buried alive, holding up an arm until it had withered, in order that their souls might be free. India understood this method of attaining a great end. Gandhi appealed to this undercurrent of Indian life. But he did more than that. He pointed out a way to use suffering for a more practical, earthly, immediate end . . . that of political, economic and social freedom for India.

"I believe that non-violence is infinitely superior to violence; forgiveness is more manly than punishment" says the calm Gandhi, speaking of Amritsar. "Forgiveness adorns a soldier. Let me not be misunderstood. Strength does not come from physical capacity. It comes from an indomitable will. A definite forgiveness would therefore mean a definite recognition of our strength.

"I am not a visionary. I claim to be a practical idealist. The religion of non-violence is not meant merely for saints. It is for the common people. Non-violence is the law of our species as violence is the law of the brute. The spirit lies dormant in the brute and he knows no might but that of physical might. The dignity of man requires a higher law.

"So I am pleading for India to practice non-violence, not because she is weak...but being conscious of her strength and power. No training in arms is necessary for realization of her strength. We may seem to need this because we think of ourselves as a mere lump of flesh. I want India to recognize that she has a soul that cannot perish and that can rise triumphant above every physical weakness and defy the physical combination of the whole world."

Is this a pacifist talking? Perhaps. A fighting pacifist! But it is not the language of a fanatic.

Having fired the soul of India with this new patriotism, Gandhi immediately put the spirit of passive resistance to work. He organized the boycott of foreign goods. He went a step further and pulled the spinning wheel out of the Indian attic and set all India to spinning its own goods so that it need not be dependent upon another nation. He not only refused to pay taxes but encouraged others to similar civil disobedience. Nor did he foolishly think his message could capture India by some mystical journey on the wings of the wind. Why should the Indian people respond enthusiastically to his boycott scheme when they could get machine-made cloth much more cheaply than the coarser homespun that he was advocating? Gandhi's own caste brothers were tradesmen, inured to oriental haggling over a penny. Therefore he had to get over to the people in dramatic form the worth and necessity of the ideal for which they were struggling.

A MASTER DRAMATIST

He accomplished the dramatization of his position in various ways. His famous march to the sea to make salt, as a

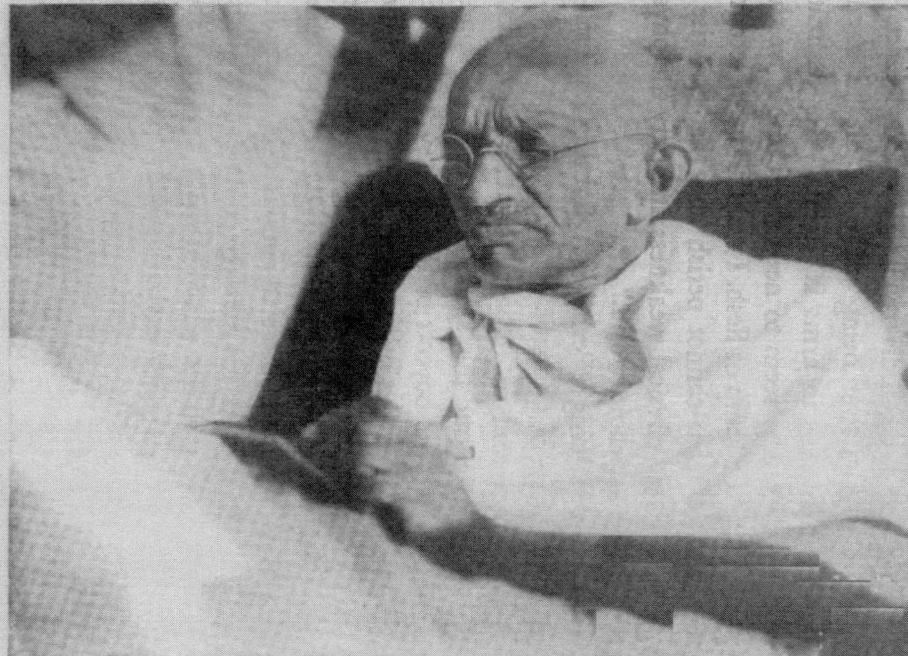

THE STATESMAN AT WORK

protest against an unjust tax, started in ridicule, but it ended on the front page of every newspaper in the world. Busy as he was with mountains of routine, he took time to spin his allotted amount every day . . . and the whirr of his spinning wheel went not only all over India but to the far corners of the earth. Which was just what Gandhi had to achieve; for to win his point he had not only to be backed by his own people, but by enlightened public opinion abroad.

I had walked hand in hand with him years before in the Indian dawn while he told me that some day he would draw the freedom loving mind of America to his standard. When I asked how, he said "I'll find a way."

He advocated the giving up of all titles and prestige conferred by the government upon Indians. Rabindranath Tagore had already thrown his knighthood back at King George's head. Thousands of Indians gave up similar though lesser honors. Gandhi himself wrapped up in tissue paper the medals, those bits of glory he had won from the government on many a battlefield, and mailed them back addressed simply "To the British Government." All these moves were dramatic. They were also the sincere acts of a patriot. And Gandhi was intelligent enough to appreciate the power of using drama to favor his difficult cause.

But he did not depend merely upon drama. He organized a counter attack against the government in the form of a patriotic society (without guns but with military precision and strict rules) a loyal society called The Volunteers. Every patriot a worker. No drones; no cowards; order; obedience, precision.

This peaceful army of young college graduates and educated youth of India were to accept the law of poverty. They were to travel third class through the country, dependent upon a very small support given directly by the people they served;

to impress upon the populace as a whole the ideals for which the movement for passive resistance stood; to teach the mobs that every crowd must be orderly, that they must school themselves in restraint. These Volunteers are at once the schoolmasters and the passive policemen of the movement. Thus Gandhi organized his country-wide army of insistent patriotism. He recruited and officered its regiments. Men; women; youth; age.

PUBLIC OPINION COUNTS

Through all these means he developed a public opinion that was at once patriotic, above caste, and united as India had never been before. He organized groups of cultured Indian women who had never before broken *purdah,* that is, passed unveiled beyond the curtain that cuts off the women's quarters from the men's in an Indian house. These women stood in the market places and were jostled by coolies; they swarmed the Mohammedan meat markets and the bazaars to point the finger of scorn at those who bought foreign goods. They blocked the entrances of government controlled saloons to prevent men from entering and ordering liquor and opium. And these mild women were so successful that when the liquor licenses for Bombay were put up at auction there was not a single bidder.

Thus were drama and organization welded by Gandhi to bring forth the new weapon of a bloodless war. Is such an organizer a mere ascetic dreamer? Or a leader of men? An impractical idealist? Or a practical statesman?

Had Gandhi organized a violent armed revolution, under the national control that he had achieved over the mind and heart of India, it would have been impossible for England to hold India at this time without the loss of somewhere between six hundred thousand and a million British soldiers. The climate of India, with the heat of the sun, the malaria, plague, smallpox, cholera; the density of the population and the capacity of the Indian people to deal silently and secretly without revealing their purposes; all these things, highly organized upon the basis of violence, would have made it impossible for Britain in this modern day, to shoot down enough people to really win. Therefore Gandhi has been the best friend of peace, and even the best friend of the government to which he is opposed, because his principles led him to organized resistance through non-violent action.

The poise of India during this past decade, 1922 to 1932, has been one of the human mysteries. It has been Gandhi who has held them firmly to the higher patriotism. These ten years of his life as leader of the great Indian movement will long stand in human history as one of the great spiritual, cultural, political, and economic developments of any nation. Here were hundreds of millions of people held in check by a thin little man in a loin cloth and spectacles. Had his people been British, American, European, or African, wild would have been their denunciation and speedy the attempted murder of their rulers. But Gandhi held India with a rein of the spirit, with the new type of revolution which he had developed. A peaceful revolution, appealing to the public opinion of an enlightened world—and therefore a practical revolution.

Is Gandhi mistaken? Has he over-estimated human nature even in our scientific era? The future alone knows. Even though his experiment fail, for the time being, Gandhi will have pointed out the next step in civilization to a blood-weary world.

CHAPTER III

INDIANS IN AFRICA

THE bloodless guns of passive resistance fought their first battle, curiously enough, in Africa, not India. Africa with its strange uncanny beauty, with its dramatic massing of blacks and whites and browns, gave to Gandhi his first real vision of India, not as his home, unchangeable and loved, but of India as she ought to be, united, revitalized, free.

An Anglicized Indian lawyer, wearing a frock coat, and a turban, with a fixed determination to make money, Gandhi came to Africa. He made his fortune, as he had planned; and then he gave it away. He left Africa an Indian reformer, with poverty as a coat, and a cloth about his loins. He landed in Durban Mr. Mohandas Karamchand Gandhi, Barrister; he went away plain Gandhi of India.

What, then, had changed him? Simply that Africa brought him to a stark realization of his identity with his own people. He found here the challenge to leadership.

I felt a thrill when I heard his story of his African vision of India. It came to him one evening as he was sitting at the mouth of a great mine watching the Indian "convict" laborers being herded to and from their work like so many cattle. Barbed wire and the bayonets of armed guards alike pricked the Indians if they strayed a step from the accustomed path. Yet these were not dangerous murderers or criminals; their chief fault was that they had not paid the head tax demanded by the government. Many of them could not pay; others had refused to work the mines until this tax, which they considered unjust and exorbitant, had been abolished. They were "criminal labor" because they were so unfortunate as to possess a conscience.

As Gandhi sat there, watching silently, an outcaste Indian boy came up out of the mine and stood by the barbed wire, blinking in the light of the setting sun. Gandhi the Hindu, a member of the *Bania* class which is entitled to wear the sacred thread of Brahma, to whom the very shadow of an outcaste was unclean, stood watching this air-starved boy breathing great gulps of the warm sweet breeze. Suddenly, quick as thought itself, the boy dodged between the legs of a big policeman, wormed his way under the barbed wire, and ran to snatch at a flower that, miraculously, had taken root in a pile of mine refuse. It was a great white fragrant flower, such as only the African sun can nurture, gorgeous, translucent, gathering up the lingering day in its clear petals.

As he stood there, his face passionately buried in this creamy whiteness, the small boy's naked brown body was etched like a sorrowful statue against the rays of the setting sun. His silent eloquent body grew and grew till it seemed to Gandhi to fill the whole sky: it was burdened, beauty-loving India herself who stood there, snatching at life.

Gandhi and the policeman reached the boy at the same instant. Even at such a moment the power of the Indian's personality, which was later to reconcile blood enemies and hold a nation in thrall, turned aside the white man's whip. Gandhi looked up into the policeman's face and then gathered the small brown outcaste into his high-caste arms.

"Don't be afraid!" said Gandhi in Gujerati. And only those who know him can imagine the flowing richness of his voice. "You are my brother. I will protect you. Out of the dark you came, yet loving beauty as I do. You are not an outcaste. I no longer belong to a higher caste. We are the same." Then he looked up again at the dazed policeman and his rare smile filled his eyes, as he said in English, "And you, too, are my brother ... though I hate the cruel thing for which you stand."

From that moment Gandhi became inevitably the reformer ... and political caste in India had heard its death knell.

It may seem strange that Gandhi had to come to Africa to see the disparity between the outcaste and the Brahman, between wealth and poverty, the ruler and the ruled. Yet it is often necessary for a man to get away from his familiar surroundings in order to see them more clearly; he gains perspective by distance.

CONSCIOUSNESS OF RACE

It was in Africa that Gandhi first realized his color ... and what it meant, not only for him but for hundreds of millions of his race. It may seem curious that neither the slums of Bombay nor of London, with both of which he was familiar, had roused him to a reformer's fury. But he had been born to accept the lordship of the white man in India as the norm of existence. A white man was a Sahib and an Indian was not and that was all there was to it. You learned the Englishman's language and ingratiated yourself with him as much as possible because he was a Sahib. The white man was on the upper end of the seesaw and the brown man with his burden was down ... that the brown man was not necessarily permanently down did not yet occur to this Indian youth.

Even in London Gandhi accepted the grinding poverty of a part of the people and the wealth of another section as the fated divisions of life. It had been so in the small native state of India where his family was one of the ruling class. Some people threw away enough to keep another family in food and clothing; other people, gaunt and haggard, were forced to whine for bread upon the streets. That was life. The poverty of India was merely that of Whitechapel developed to the *n*th degree. So Gandhi went away from the slums of London comparatively untouched.

But no sooner did he set foot upon the soil of Africa than he found out what it meant to be a brown man. That he was a graduate of universities; that he was here at a good salary to take part in an important legal case made no difference; here he was simply a "coolie". Nothing more! The same Aryan blood might flow in his veins as in those of the Europeans; but his mistake was that his skin was not white.

In this country, moreover, he observed, all those who had big palaces, money, hotels, who were allowed to ride in the front seats of tram cars, and attend the theatres and cathedrals, were white; and all those who had nothing were brown or black. This was a new perspective for him. It started him questioning not only what was wrong in Africa, but whether the ruling classes in India, both brown and white, English and Brahman, were wrong in their attitudes of superiority.

Gandhi's experience with the ruling white race in Africa increased this doubt. He bought a first-class ticket from Durban to Pretoria, but since three white passengers objected to a "coolie" in their compartment, the conductor told Gandhi he would have to move back into a third-class or van compartment. Gandhi refused and was put off the train, bag and baggage, to shiver through a chilly night . . . and to think. The next day, riding in a coach where he was not allowed to sit inside with the white passengers but had to stay up with the coachman, the conductor who wanted to smoke, came up to him and said,

"Sammy, you sit on this, I want to sit near the driver"... and the conductor threw a dirty piece of sacking on the floor at his feet.

Gandhi refused, and was boxed and beaten for his pains until another white passenger interfered. When, bewildered and lonely under such treatment in a strange land, Gandhi went to the sort of hotel to which his business standing entitled him, he was laughed at and informed there was "no room." He was finally admitted to a small hotel in Pretoria but told he would have to eat his meals alone in his room lest he annoy the other guests.

He began to inquire into the status of Indians in Pretoria and discovered that no Indian was allowed to be out on the streets after nine in the evening without written permission from his master. But Gandhi had no "master" from whom to get such a pass, and his business often kept him out late. What was he to do? An English barrister to whom he applied for such a license proved to be a man from his own Inn or court in London! Both the Englishman and the Indian were indignant. But what was to be done? Here was a case where law superseded justice.

Another day when Gandhi was walking innocently along, a Boer policeman officiously kicked him off the path. When the Indian, breathless, asked what he had done that was wrong, the policeman informed him that the footpaths were for the whites, not "coolies". A white friend of Gandhi's who happened to be passing explained to the Boer who Gandhi was and insisted that the policeman apologize. But Gandhi, brushing himself off, said earnestly, "It is not necessary; I have already forgiven him."

Gandhi had forgiven the policeman, but he had not forgotten. He listened to the stories of his Indian friends telling of similar treatment and when he went back to India on a visit, wrote an article describing how the Indians were treated in South Africa, not mentioning his own ills, but explaining the general situation. He also attacked the Asiatic Exclusion Act as illegal and unjust legislation. The South African whites were so enraged that when Gandhi came back to Durban to pursue his lawsuit, he was nearly killed on his way up from the dock by an angry white mob. The bravery of the wife of the English chief of police, who saw his predicament, and walked along the streets with him—a companion, in the teeth of the snarling mob—was all that saved his life.

In the face of such experiences, it would have been easily understandable if Gandhi had turned bitterly against the whites. But he did not. One time in his home I listened to his intimate and plaintive reminiscences of these sad days. It was unconsciously in the chastened spirit of the one who first said "Father forgive them, for they know not what they do." His principle of *Ahimsa* which he had learned at his mother's knee, not only forbade his killing any white person: it counselled against hatred of any living being. "For" says Gandhi "hatred is a form of violence. It is a wrong state of mind whether or not it is expressed by acts of violence." So he went calmly on making white friends, visiting with them, discussing philosophies of life, and learning new lessons in practical politics.

PROSPERITY

Gandhi's law business began to prosper. But curiously fewer and fewer of his cases got to the court room. Most of them were settled amicably out of court, through Gandhi's personal persuasion. Even then the power of his personality which was to sway India's millions was evident. "I came to realize" he said "that the true function of the lawyer was to unite parties driven asunder." A process which would seem soon to shut off any necessity of lawyers at all! But it did not work that way. Gandhi's legal calendar began to be so crowded that he took on four and then five clerks in his law office, and his income grew by leaps and bounds. All he had to do was to sit tight and in a few years he would have piled up for himself a life competence.

But the very understanding and sympathy which made him so successful in settling legal disputes would not let him rest while the indentured Indians in Africa were groaning their way to bewildered graves.

The history of indentured Indian labor in Africa depicts the curiously ironical development of an empire that offers citizenship with one hand, and with the other snatches away legal rights till the brown man finds himself with fewer privileges, socially and commercially, than the alien who lives next door. My own eyes were to see these facts all too bitterly more than a decade later.

It is the panic of race consciousness, the white man's fear that he may not be able to hold his own against the brown and black man in Africa that is responsible for such extreme attitudes. Yet so strongly is Africa his, by right of armed conquest, that it is the white man who is known as the "South African" while the Indian is a "coolie" and the indigenous black man a "native". This is true in spite of, or perhaps because of, the fact that the black majority is still overwhelming. The racial divisions in the Union of South Africa are approximately as follows: White, one million, five hundred thousand; Indians, two hundred thousand; mixed blood, seven hundred thousand; blacks, six million.

Both the European and the Indian were originally aliens in South Africa; but the white man fought his way by force of arms while the Indians came at the invitation or rather the lure of the white planter. Just about the time that America was struggling to shake herself free of slavery through Civil War, the white planters in Africa were trying to solve the problem

© Keystone-Underwood

THE YOUNG BARRISTER OF LONDON AND SOUTH AFRICA

of developing huge sugar plantations and digging vast mines with the shifting black labor then available.

The native black man still had plenty of land of his own which he could cultivate to suit his own ends and social needs. He could stick a yam or two into the fertile soil and have a harvest sufficient for his immediate needs. He preferred the tribal campfire to blistering hours in the white man's cane fields . . . so why should he not desert an employer when he wanted to go back to his own home? The result of such nomadic psychology was that the planter often found himself facing wholesale desertion by black labor at the precious moment of harvest. The cane was spoiling in his fields. What was to be done?

INDENTURED LABORERS

Someone conceived the brilliant plan of sending to India for agricultural labor. The Indian farmer was well known as one of the most thrifty in the world. He could raise a crop with fewer drops of water than any other agriculturist because his climate had forced him to learn to do it. More than that, he was a patient dependable worker, whose word was his bond. The result of this inspiration was that, with the consent of the British government in India, recruiting agents from South Africa untied little bags of gold nuggets before the dark wondering eyes of the Indian villagers. Most of these humble farmers had never held a piece of gold in their hands before. They were told that not only were the streams of Africa running with bright gold, but that if the Indians signed up for agriculture in Africa, at the end of their term of service they would be able to purchase a homestead of their own in this marvelous new country where they could live in peace and plenty for the rest of their lives. What wonder then that thousands of villagers put their thumb prints to the agricultural agreements. Thus indentured labor in South Africa began.

The Indian fulfilled his part of the bargain faithfully. As the *Natal Mercury* of 1865 reports:

"Had it not been for the coolie (Indian) labor we should certainly not have had it to say that our sugar export increased from £26,000 in 1863 to £100,000 in 1864, and has prospects of a greater increase before it. Had it not been for the coolie labor we should not hear of coffee plantations springing up on all hands and of the prosperity of older ones being sustained solely through the agency of the East India man."[1]

The Indian now began to plant little truck gardens of his own on the outskirts of the white towns (the Indians were always segregated in colonies of their own), and was prosperous in a mild way. But these transplanted people yearned often for the ghee (clarified butter), the Indian sweetmeats, spices, curries and rice of their Indian villages, and the women missed the trinkets and the inexpensive jewels they used to prize and display at home. So, Indian traders came.

Curiously, not only the Indians, but the native Africans seemed to prefer dealing with these traders to buying from the whites. And yet it was not so strange. The Indian is willing to spend more time bargaining than is the European. The African is fond of spending a pleasant hour over his purchases (and why not when they are bought with days of sweaty toil under a burning sun?). Even the poor Europeans began to buy from the Indian trader because his goods were cheaper than those of the white merchant. Moreover the Indian was willing to give long credit and easy terms of payment and seldom if ever took a client to court. All these were telling

---

[1] Bhawani Dayal Sannyasi and Benarsidas Chaturvedi, *A Report on the Emigrants Repatriated to India under the Assisted Emigration Scheme from South Africa, and On the Problem of Returned Emigrants from All Colonies.*

arguments in the Indian merchant's favor. He required no other advertising. Consequently many of these traders grew very prosperous—so prosperous that the whites began to get uneasy.

What happens when a brown man can afford a Rolls Royce! Is that not a direct insult to those white people who still have to run Fords? There is something wrong somewhere, argued the whites. We must look into this matter. They did! To such purpose that the legislative adoption of a series of anti-Asiatic Acts aggravated the disparity between the whites and browns. Here was social, legal and commercial discrimination.

While arguing that the Indian traders were too wealthy, the white man began also to complain that on the contrary, the standard of living of the Indian laborers was too low for competition. But was this standard entirely the Indian's doing? Who could maintain a very high standard of living upon $12 a month? The barracks or living quarters provided by the plantations or mills for these workers did not foster cleanliness or social improvement. They were (and are) ramshackle huts made of mud, brick, or tin, or of all three. As one European remarked ruefully, "The only respectable thing about them is the whitewash on the outside."

RACE SEGREGATION

The Indians were segregated in sections swampy or otherwise undesirable, in which the Europeans themselves would not live. The Indian laborers' toil had made of Natal such a thing of beauty that it was now called "The Garden of Africa," . . . but they themselves were thrown out of the garden into the back alley. Ghetto districts grew up, and even here there was small encouragement for an Indian to own and improve property, because at any moment the government might condemn this section and tell the Indians they must find another place to live. In some cities, such as Johannesburg, Indians were refused by law the right to own any property at all. Finally an anti-Asiatic bill proposed taking away from the Indian even the little gardens which he had purchased outside the city limits.

The educated Indians began to ask themselves, "What advantage does a citizen of the British Empire have? South Africa is a part of the Empire; India is also a part of the Empire. Yet an Indian in South Africa does not have as many privileges as a citizen of America, or of France, or of Germany, or of Japan!"

The Christian churches and social agencies in South Africa join with the government in this curious policy of offering the white man's ideals with one hand and denying Christian principles with the other. We can hardly be surprised that the brown man questions either our sincerity or our sanity when in one breath we offer him Christ, and with the next breath drive him from our white church door.

When I was in South Africa in 1925, I had occasion to discuss an important matter with a brilliant young Indian, a graduate with honors from a British university. I suggested that he meet me in the lobby of the Y. M. C. A. for a conference.

"I'm sorry, but I'm afraid they won't let me in there," he said quietly.

I laughed at him.

"Come along. I'll be expecting you." I went to the director of the Y. M. C. A. and told him what I had done. He was embarrassed but said that because of public opinion no Indian could be allowed in his lobby. I went back to my hotel and left word to have my friend sent up to my room immediately he arrived. But he was not allowed to enter the lobby to ask for me at the hotel desk. I myself had to go out in the street to talk to him. As I stood there on the sidewalk, almost speechless, he said without rancor,

"There's a Mohammedan mosque just down the street. They'll let us in."

The only public place that an Indian Christian college graduate and a white Christian Bishop could find for a Christian visit was on the cushioned floor of a Mohammedan mosque!

This was not an isolated instance. Over and over again Indian friends of Mrs. Fisher and myself were refused permission to enter the sanctuaries and auditoriums where I was speaking in various cities of Natal and the Transvaal. One church official even cancelled a dinner party which he had arranged in our honor because of "the disgraceful attempt of your Indian friends to force their way into a white church." What had happened was that fourteen well dressed Indians, Christians, Hindus, and Mohammedans, hearing that I who had newly come from their home country would speak that Sunday morning, had come quietly, orderly, respectfully to a public Christian service. They gladly sat in the vestibule, but that was too much for my big white friend. How big? How white? How friendly?

The knotting of this already tightening situation came when a tax of fifteen dollars was proposed to be collected from every indentured laborer upon the completion of his contract in Africa. This was an amount he could not possibly save out of his small wages. Therefore as soon as his services were ended, he could be deported back to India.

But the Indian did not want to be deported. He had been promised a chance to buy land and build a home and he wanted to build it. He had grown used to the climate of Africa and did not want to return to over-populated India.

His children had been born in Africa and knew no other customs or ways of living. Why should he have to go away any more than a white man? The Europeans too were foreigners. So long as the black man who owned the continent by right of birth did not wish to get rid of him, why should the Indian be driven out? The answer was of course, "Because the white man is strong enough in force of arms to send you away as he brought you . . . when it suits his convenience."

It was this final overwhelming tax that brought Gandhi with his weapon of passive resistance to the aid of the indentured laborer. But the Indian lawyer had been too keen minded not to see which way the wind was blowing. He had been quietly getting himself ready for generalship as well as planning out his campaign.

MORAL BULLETS FOR SPIRITUAL MACHINE GUNS

The bullets for his machine guns of the spirit were to come from the new vow of *Satyagraha* which he first took in South Africa, the vow of allegiance to truth. This vow meant not only loyalty to truth from a subjective viewpoint—that is, that he himself would never lie: but it meant also an insistence, an objective insistence, upon the application of truth to the problems of daily life. "If a principle is worth anything, it's worth living" says Gandhi.

That is where his real contest with our western civilization begins. He does not say that we do not know the truth: we had the Sermon on the Mount before he found it. But we were brought up to believe that while these principles of Christ, to love one another, to turn the other cheek, were ideally lustrous, they were not practical. Like a wedding dress, they were to be donned for special occasions when we didn't have to do the ordinary grubbing work of life.

"You know the truth," he says, "but you do not practise it. You prefer the bloody days of the Old Testament to the emerging power of the essential Christian doctrine, that love, indeed, may conquer the earth."

"What then is truth?" he asks. Truth in its essence is not violent. It has a quiet growth. It is the still small voice. Truth cannot be hatred: it must be love. To practise truth means that you renounce hatred and practise love. In its full implication the vow of *Satyagraha* means peaceful, non-violent, non-resentful insistence upon the practise of truth. Could such a doctrine have gripped the consciousness of any other nation in the world except India, already experienced in the strength of endurance? It took an Indian statesman and an Indian nation to show the power of directed will.

The implications of such a personal and political creed as Gandhi had here developed and began to preach in his newspaper, *"Indian Opinion,"* established in Africa in 1904, are obvious. The way was not only paved for passive resistance but for the later economic boycott in India.

A passion for living the truth paved the way for many changes in Gandhi's personal life. He must acknowledge and obey truth now and in the future, in whatever guise he might find it.

SEXUAL CONTINENCE

One of the first results of this attitude was that he took the vow of sexual continence. He confessed to himself that in his early life he had had excessive sexual indulgence, even though within the bonds of matrimony. Indulgence, he reasoned, was in itself a form of violence; violence to his own nature, as child marriage in general had done violence to all India. The practise of truth meant that such violence must cease; for he had by now come to identify truth with the gaining of all human rights for the Indians. He would begin this fight for truth in South Africa. But he would not be free to work for any such cause so long as he was hampered by family ties which made him fear prison or similar sacrifices. Very well, then, he would give up family privileges and duties and thus free himself to work for the cause of truth. He talked this matter over with his wife; and by mutual agreement they added to *Satyagraha,* the vow of chastity.

But this vow of chastity implied no ascetic, monastic withdrawal from the world; on the contrary it was taken precisely that they might serve more freely in the world. Therefore it was required of all fellow-workers who came to the cooperative colony which they founded at Phoenix, Natal.

I visited Monilal Gandhi, a faithful son of his father, at this Tolstoy Colony in 1925. It was not established as a sort of joint monastery and nunnery. It was a cooperative farming scheme where each member should by the toil of his own hands earn his daily vegetables and rice; and where each man, woman and child should have the chance to work out his system of ideals, of truth. In this way he could go back into the world to work intelligently for the truth, instead of firing his guns unaimed like so many half-cocked reformers. It speaks volumes for the practical wisdom of Gandhi that this was his plan of action.

Any army, even a peaceful one, needs training in the use of ammunition, especially when the bullets are moral truth, and this is exactly what the members of the Phoenix Farm got. Here *"Indian Opinion"* was and still is published, and here the Gandhi group gathered to discuss and outline their plan of attack upon organized armed force. Here the general staff of passive resistance had its first council of war; and established its first headquarters.

Gandhi had been greatly influenced, not only by Tolstoy's

books, but by his personality. When Tolstoy heard that Gandhi was really trying out the principle of passive resistance as a practical political force, the Russian wrote letters of encouragement to the Hindu. The impact of Tolstoy's "*The Kingdom of God is Within You*" upon Gandhi's mind did much to crystallize his ideals into action. He came to realize that he must win a definite victory over himself before he could conquer others for his cause. Just as Tolstoy found that when he had devoted his life to being the kind of Christian he thought Christ wanted him to be he lost all desire for his old imperial licentious ways, so the Hindu found that once he gave himself up to the search for truth, smaller personal passions were swallowed up. The same God brooded over India, Africa, Russia.

So reasoned Gandhi. Already he was ceasing to be the dapper, self-willed young lawyer who had come to Africa. He was reaching out after the constructive idealism of Mahatma Gandhi. But he had still a long way to go.

The next step was to take the vow of equality with the poor peasants of India and of the indentured Indians in Africa. This implied poverty. Already Gandhi had used up his not inconsiderable resources in his fight to arouse intelligent public opinion on the status of Indians in Africa. It was of necessity as well as choice that the colony at Phoenix became self supporting, and walked cheerfully back and forth from town, a distance of thirty miles.

The vow of poverty was necessary also in view of the thousands of illiterate indentured Indians who were flocking in almost embarrassing numbers to Gandhi's standard. These people had little or no money and must exist in the simplest possible manner. So Gandhi began to experiment with diet to see how little a man could live upon and still be happy and well.

Gandhi has been first and last an experimenter. He refuses to adopt an idea until he has tried it out in the laboratory of personal experience. In this sense he is as much a modern scientist as Edison...only that most of Edison's ideas worked themselves out in electrical force while Gandhi's dealt with moral force. Not all Gandhi's early ideas have proven the best in the world; neither were Edison's, who once tried to make his boyhood chum fly by giving him seidlitz powders! But as Edison, up to his death, patiently boiled weed after weed to try to find the proper combination for synthetic rubber, so Gandhi tried out food after food to find what was necessary for simple healthy existence.

He already, because of his religion, ate no meat. He tried to live on uncooked vegetables to find out if he could save his poverty-stricken followers the cost of fuel. He also tried going without salt. Neither of these plans worked, so he quit them. He tried eating fruit only, and found he had to have milk. So his diet finally resolved itself into fruit, cereals, and milk. He rose every morning at four and took a long walk which not only gave him a chance to think alone before the confusion of the day began, but also kept him in the glow of health.

"You white folk eat too much!" Gandhi once said laughingly to me, contrasting his thin body with my comfortably padded bulk. "Then you have to go to a drug store and get some pepsin or mint. I eat food that doesn't need so much attention, and I save in three ways—in time, expense, and drugs!"

Is this a fanatic? Perhaps. But a wise one. He knows that the struggle to which he has set himself is no brief skirmish, but a long drawn out battle. If he is to make the boycott in India successful, he must construct a program by means of which he and his followers can subsist on meager food, scant clothing and inexpensive pleasures. This first stripping down to get ready for a battle of long endurance began here on the Phoenix Farm.

A DRAMATIC EXTREMIST

His continence, his diet, his poverty, were arms for a new kind of battle. They were also sheer drama. For Gandhi is perhaps the greatest living dramatist. He is not dramatic, however, in the way a good publicist plans his campaign, merely for effect. He is naturally an extremist, and an extremist is always dramatic. He was that kind of a man back in Africa two decades before the newspapers discovered him; he hasn't changed his make-up since the time when taking a glass of goat's milk for breakfast made front page news in every paper on earth.

Thus if Gandhi believes sexual indulgence wrong, he swings way over to entire continence. If he thinks the poor overtaxed, he refuses to pay any taxes at all. If he thinks his country wrong in using any violence against England, he not only preaches and practises non-violence himself, but when sporadic violence breaks out, takes the blame upon himself and fasts in penance till it nearly kills him. If he thinks militarism wrong he swings clear over to no fighting at all. If he seeks to identify himself with the life of the peasant, he leaps to the dramatic ultimate and wears a loin cloth.

He is not a showman. He simply believes passionately in his "truth"; he not only talks about it, he lives it. He dramatizes his idea by giving a living example of what he means. That is why he is such good copy for the newspapers; for all successful news is full of images, examples, life, not disembodied ideas. It is front page copy when a politician actually lives as though he means what he says.

This dramatic sincerity, this passion for truth wherever found, caused Gandhi to drop his barriers of caste at the mouth of the African mine when he drew the outcaste boy into his arms. He saw that slavery was not a matter of color; the Brahman held the outcaste in social slavery. It was an imperialistic state of mind that produced slavery. Gandhi did not hesitate to attack, therefore, the slave mind within his own Hindu society.

"Slave-holders ourselves! We have no right to quarrel with our own masters if we are not prepared unconditionally to enfranchise our own slaves!" he told his followers when they objected to an outcaste family being taken into the *Ashram*, "We must have no lines of either caste or creed."

To emphasize this point Gandhi always goes out of his way to do physical labor—the labor of the hands so despised by the orthodox Brahman. During the march of the strikers to the Transvaal, Gandhi himself helped to act as camp scavenger. He not only allowed outcastes in his *Ashram* at Ahmedabad, but he himself adopted an outcaste girl as his legal daughter. He spins daily in order that he may constantly remind himself and his co-workers that to serve is not a lowering of caste. "Let him that is greatest among you be the servant of all."

Gandhi differs radically from other great reformers in that he refuses to become bitter; and in his astonishing capacity to see good in the enemy, while hating the injustice for which he stands. To Gandhi it was not the armed power of the American Civil War, but the idealism behind it which was the great force. It was not Lincoln the soldier but Lincoln the idealist who led an army to victory and banished slavery from America. Gandhi thinks the time has come for a new kind of battle, a struggle of ideals against bayonets.

He soon had need of all his weapons, for the first battle of passive resistance was upon him. When to the threatened tax of fifteen dollars upon indentured laborers, was added the decision of a Judge that all marriages in South Africa were illegal unless celebrated by Christian rites, the match that was to light the South African conflagration had been struck. This decision challenged the honor of every Hindu, Mohammedan, and Zoroastrian marriage in South Africa. The women rose up in arms. When the home is set on fire it does not take long to ignite a nation.

Gandhi held a council of war at Phoenix, and it was decided that the women of the *Ashram* should make the first try at arrest as passive resisters, thus registering their protest against prevailing conditions. Failing that, the women were to go to Newcastle to endeavor to enlist the miners for passive resistance. The women did this stirring up of the miners with eager thoroughness; and when the women were put in jail and two of them died as a result, strike followed strike as mine after mine joined the ranks of the resisters. The wave of unarmed protest grew till the government had to work overtime to put as many of the offenders as possible into jail.

The workers tried no sabotage; they did not even strike back when attacked by whips or guns; they just silently refused to work. Finally when the jails threatened to burst, the government took over the mines as auxiliary prisons; and made the Indians work at the point of bayonets. Forced labor is far from satisfactory as the French were to find later in the Ruhr. And such military slavery would hardly quiet the remainder of the Indians.

The successful march of Gandhi and his brave, almost penniless and motley army from Durban to the Transvaal, where they knew they would be arrested for crossing the border without permission, is worthy an epic of Homer. Here were educated, sensitive intellectuals from the colleges of England, India, and America, and from the Phoenix *Ashram;* here also were bewildered but immovable farmers and miners, burning with the insult set upon their persons, homes and families. Here were honest men; thieves scenting booty; wise men and cunning; all pouring by the hundreds and thousands into Gandhi's camp.

Here also were the women. Women warriors of the new army of peace! With their babies on their hips or tugging at their skirts. Children dying at their mothers' breasts from exposure; children falling into rivers and drowning. But still the flood of patient enduring India flowed steadily toward the camp of passive resistance, trusting to God and Gandhi. Some of them had even sold their small possessions, thinking this was to be a long drawn out struggle, and had brought along their little to buy food. But how to feed the rest? How to keep order in this vast concourse, how to protect them from disease?

"I had no means of housing them; the sky was the only roof over our heads," Gandhi explains. "But I was confident the trader class (wealthy Indians) would not fail to feed us. The traders of Newcastle supplied cooking pots and bags of rice. Other things were showered upon us—rice, vegetables, condiments. Contributions exceeded my expectations. Not all were ready to go to jail; but all felt for the cause." [1]

Yet it was dangerous, he knew, to try to keep so large and so mixed an "army" in one place without employment. What was he to do with them? With his usual practicality he thinks out a scheme before he goes to bed; it is none other than to march this "army" at once thirty-six miles to the Tansvaal border where the authorities will arrest them . . . and thus, he remarks, they "will be safely deposited in jail!"

That is exactly what he did . . . deposited his army safely in jail. And, doubtless breathing a sigh of relief, he too went

---

[1] Andrews, C. F.: *Autobiography of Gandhi.* (New York, 1930.)

to jail. It must have been a comparative rest cure after the siege he had just been through.

But though Gandhi's passive resistance had practically paralyzed the mines of South Africa and interfered with business everywhere, he showed throughout no vindictive spirit. He even sent some of his workers to help harvest a sugar crop that was obviously spoiling, and refused to side with railway strikers who were merely out to harass the government. "We want justice . . . not retribution" he said.

How could the white men ruthlessly shoot down an enemy who thus assisted them? It was all very puzzling to know what to do. Gandhi won his chief points. In return for his agreement that there was to be no more Indian immigration, the whites repudiated the unjust tax upon indentured laborers, the slur upon their homes, and other legal discriminations. The Indians were gradually released from their jail boarding houses, returning to their homes and work.

The battle for equality in South Africa was not yet completely won. The Indian might still be called a "coolie"; but he had gained self respect, and had learned the use of new victorious weapons.

Thus ended the first battle of passive resistance . . . and thus began the new chapter of Mahatma Gandhi, the fighting soul of India.

CHAPTER IV

THE FIGHTING PACIFIST

"Rags! Rags! Shall I wear
Straw! Straw! Shall I eat
For the sake of thy life,
My Motherland.

Into the street
Neath trampling feet
I cast all fame,
To serve thy name
O heart's dear flame
My Motherland." [1]

SOMEWHERE behind a closed window in Bombay, a woman was singing this battle hymn of passive resistance. But in the streets of the city there was no singing. Only silence.

The terrible silence of India! I have experienced it. Thousands of soft feet slipping through the warm dust, pliant sandals and slippers making no sound on the pavement. No sound; no voice. You were alone on a street corner of Bombay; then, suddenly you turned your head, and all India was there at your shoulder. All day long on June 21st, 1930, the crowds of Indians had been gathering against the strict orders of the constabulary that there must be no national meetings or parades. The people had begun coming in the early morning, yet so silent was their approach that before

---

[1] Winslow, J. C., *Biography of Narayan Tilak*. (Calcutta, 1923.) A free rendering by F. B. F.

the government knew it, every square yard of the main avenue of Bombay was covered by a vast human sea of bodies.

Silence, absolute, menacing, more terrible than trumpets. It was only when the police put up machine guns on the street corner and threatened the mob if they did not disperse, that India began its march.

"If you come as far as the corner, we will shoot!"

The message was brought to the man heading the parade, by an armed soldier, the clatter of his horse's feet beating defiantly against the menacing quiet.

"We will fire to kill!"

"Very well, fire."

With a sigh of released patience, the crowd began to move slowly, relentlessly, proudly, towards the deadly corner. The leaders held their heads high... till the rat tat tat of machine guns sent them bowing awkwardly into the dust. The English had fired as they had promised.

Still there was little confusion; only the gasps of the wounded and dying, their clumsy twitchings in the street. The leaders were gone. Would the crowd march on? Silently, slowly, yet as certainly as an incoming tide that cannot be stemmed, the next in rank stepped over the dead and came towards the guns. Once more the stutter of guns, the gleam of metal under a blazing sun. More men whirled, fell, coughing blood, clutched helplessly at their bursting stomachs, and then fell dead. But still the steady stream came on, more and more men, more and more women; stern, implacable, ready to die. It could not be true! but it was. It was a scene out of Dante's hell, imagined, not to be believed.

"I say. This is terrible. We can't do this, Captain!"

It was the young English lieutenant speaking. "Can't we move the guns up to the next corner?"

There was sweat on the Captain's forehead.

"Yes. Move them up. And warn the Indians that if they stop now we will not shoot. But they must not come to the next corner."

The crowd was told . . . but it still marched on. Guns were hurried to another corner. Still the crowd swept silently forward. What was to be done? All Bombay could not be slaughtered. "What can we do to get you to stop?" the English officer called.

The low voice of the Indian leader stirred the thick layer of Indian silence for the first time.

"So long as you point your guns at us, we will march. Rescind your order against our meeting, take away your guns . . . and we will disperse."

"But that would be to surrender!"

"Very well then. We will march till every one of these thousands is dead."

It was India demanding a chance to be heard. The guns were removed, the crowd melted away like magic, lifting up the wounded and burying their dead. But the voice of silent India had been heard on her own streets of Bombay.[1]

Such passive resistance methods would not have been successful in the days of Attila the Hun, or even of Jaime, the Spanish conquistador, who only 700 years ago burned his Majorcan heathen captives in Christian oil. The effectiveness of these methods of the Indian passive resisters today depends upon enlightened public opinion, upon the verdict of a modern world which labels wholesale slaughter of unarmed men as belonging to the days of barbarism, rather than to 1932.

Moreover, a new international will to peace had been born from the womb of the World War. In 1919 the whole white world was weary of guns. Hardly a home in England, France,

---

[1] Farson, Negley, *Chicago Daily News,* July 2, 1930.

Belgium, Germany, but had its crape upon the door; even America had not escaped unscathed. The years from 1917 to 1919 had been rather a war of muddy endurance than of enthusiastic combat. The gilt edge of battle had been rubbed off and the world was clutching at the safety of peace. At this psychological moment came Gandhi with the first practical plan of gaining national ends through non-violent effort that the world had ever seen.

Fifty years ago such a passive resistance movement would not have created a stir. A year before the World War it would probably not have succeeded. Certainly it would not have attracted such international interest. But now a world which had crawled home to lick its scars, was interested in a constructive method for peace. Almost any plan of peace, for the moment. The will to peace was for the most part planless, diaphanous, oratorical, as polite and aimless as a lecture at a Friday morning women's club. But it was there. Gandhi took this will to peace and shaped it into a practical political weapon.

DIVIDING AND RULING

The first thing Gandhi did with this new idealism was to use it as a wedge to divide English public opinion. He appealed to the war-weary people of England by his use of non-violence, and in so doing he turned the ancient British principle . . . "Divide and rule" . . . which England had so long manipulated so neatly among the many factions of her eastern possessions, against England itself.

This new peaceful war was not entirely a war of India against Great Britain. It was essentially a war between the idealists in England and India against the military terrorists of England and the landed Indian rulers. If Gandhi could keep English public opinion divided upon the Indian policy, his passive resistance movement had a chance. But this was not an entirely selfish policy. It was to England's advantage as well as India's. For if Gandhi had not kept India from violence, she would, without doubt, have been washed in a wave of bloodshed that would have wiped out the very memory of the Mutiny of 1857.

The World War had also played its part in preparing Indian public opinion for non-violence, and a return to the essentially Indian doctrine of *Ahimsa*—a reluctance to kill any living thing. Thousands of Indian troops in the war had had a chance to see what modern fighting on a large scale was like . . . and they did not like it. It was contrary to their very national fibre. Their gift was for enduring suffering; not for causing it.

I once stood beside an Indian friend of Gandhi's on the deserted battlefield at Ypres. Yesterday the troops had been there; today there was only death inhabiting the shell holes; and desolation. The dugouts and trenches were filled with water—turgid bloody pools upon which floated the swollen entrails of nameless men. Near us, in a tangle of barbed wire, lay a horse with his head completely blown off, like some bloody nightmare, and beside him the human rider turned a face of frozen horror and surprise to the unseeing sky. There were other corpses. But somehow, more terrible than all this slaughter, which seemed curiously inhuman and unreal, was the broken figure on a wooden crucifix which hung over the gun-blasted road. There He hung . . . a Christ with broken, hollow skirts, still clinging to His silent Cross.

Suddenly the Indian at my side began to scream. He struck the resounding wood with his clenched knuckles. It rattled.

"I cannot endure it!" he cried. "The hollowness of this Christ! And you a Christian, walking with me over these bloody fields. You wanted me to study at your college, to learn of you. Is this, then, Christ? This is not even civilized! I am going back to Gandhi and tell him what hypocrites he and all of us are. He has been recruiting soldiers for this war. Yet his is the way of truth! This is not the way out!" The next week he set sail for India.

At this same moment Gandhi himself was coming to a similar conclusion in Poona. Gandhi was saying sadly to his friends,

"I am sorry I had anything to do with this war. I believed Woodrow Wilson's dream; that it was a war to end war. But I see now that force can never banish force." He turned to a European standing near, "It was your own Cross method you should have used," he said slowly. "The remedy was ready at your hand and you would not use it. But India will use it." He said this at a time when even the missionaries in India, shaken by a Christian world in chaos, were beginning to doubt if they had any message for India. They had gone there, not only to teach Christ, but western ways of civilization . . . and the whole edifice of the white man's building was tottering about their ears. It took a Hindu to point the Christians to the Cross and say, "There is the real remedy for war! There is power not only to save, but to rule the world."

It is useless to say that when you thus bring religion into politics you become an impractical dreamer. Religion *is* politics in India today; passive resistance is more than a political movement; it is the unshakable belief of India that the will, the spirit, is stronger than the force of arms. And in reaching down into the heart of India and lifting up idealism to practicality, Gandhi became the idol of a nation.

Emerson said of Napoleon that he was the great ideal soul of France, and that every Frenchman was just a little Napoleon. This characterizes Gandhi's relationship to India today. The qualities of his character, the moral weapons that he uses, the spirit of his daily living, represent what India wants to be. Therefore they follow him. It is doubtful if in any other country in the world he could have attained such acknowledged leadership. He would have been considered too much of a dreaming idealist to be followed in practical western politics. Had his people not been like him, to ever so small an extent, they would never have given him the overwhelming response he has had, a response unique in modern loyalties.

And if Gandhi was shrewd enough to use the idealism of the English to help him win his point, is that not proof that he is sufficiently practical to be trusted with leadership in rebuilding a nation?

AN ANCIENT BLOODLESS EMPIRE

This was not India's first experiment in the rule of peace. Two hundred years before Christ and two hundred years after Buddha, the Emperor Asoka had built and established an empire identical in geographical extent with modern India. He had built up his power by the sword; but the sight of the blood-stained battlefield of Kalinga had turned him to peace. He adopted the pacific policies of Buddha so thoroughly that he scrapped his armies, threw away his swords and spears, and ruled for forty years through the non-violent power of love. After that Asoka's only army was composed of Buddhist priests who spread Buddhism in Burma, Tibet, Ceylon, China, Korea, Japan, and portions of Asia Minor; an army of indefatigable idealists whose influence is felt, even yet, around the world.

But Gandhi brought back from Africa an aggressive, militant pacifism, adapted to this modern day. It was the old Hindu and Buddhist ideal of *Ahimsa,* of suffering, yet doing no harm to any living being. It was more. Ancient *Ahimsa* was negative. Gandhi's *Ahimsa* was a positive, aggressive, political weapon. "Insist upon truth by loving argument, by the testimony of your own life. Once you are assured of the truth, refuse to recant, even to death!" This was Gandhi of India. Harmlessness, plus insistence upon the truth, did not make a bullet-proof combination . . . but it defeated the British that day at Bombay.

Gandhi, contrary to popular western belief, is no visionary, counselling cowardice, and cringing submission to the will of another. "Where there is only a choice between cowardice and violence, I advise violence" he says. "I cultivate the quiet courage of dying without killing, but to him who has not this courage, I advise that of killing and of being killed, rather than that of shamefully fleeing from danger. For he who runs away commits mental violence. He runs away because he has not the courage to be killed while he kills. I would risk violence a thousand times rather than emasculation of race. I would rather have India resort to arms to defend her honor than that she should in a cowardly manner become or remain a helpless victim to her own dishonor.

"But I believe that non-violence is infinitely superior to violence,—forgiveness more manly than punishment. Abstinence from violence is forgiveness only when there is power to punish. It is meaningless when it pretends to proceed from a helpless creature. A mouse cannot forgive a cat for eating it. I do not believe India to be helpless. Non-violence does not mean meek submission to the will of the evil-doer, but the putting of one's whole soul against the will of the tyrant. Working under this law of our being, it is possible for a single individual to defy the whole might of an unjust Empire and lay the foundation for that Empire's fall or its regeneration."

Gandhi knew war. I have heard from his lips the most graphic descriptions of battlefields, troops, spoils, victories, and defeats. He had proved himself no coward. He refused from principle to carry arms, but he had carried a stretcher through the thick of the fighting during the Boer War when the Englishman was fighting the Boer. Also during the Zulu rebellion, when the white man was fighting the black, Gandhi often walked twenty to thirty miles a day under the blazing sun of Africa, carrying the wounded, patching up the destruction that war had made. He knew the cold singing of bullets, the scream of the dying. He had received the Kaiser-i-Hind medal, and other honors from the British Government for his African services. He had been in England at the outbreak of the war. But somewhere amid the silences of the African night, he had come to the conclusion that war was wrong; it took human life; besides it did not pay; it was futile. The outcome of the European war confirmed this belief.

"War does not even help the victor" Gandhi decided. "It makes him brutal and proud; nothing is added to his culture, or even to his gold. All he has left is debts and empty homes. And war certainly does not aid the loser. He is resentful, filled with the bitter meat of hatred, developing a slave mentality and an incapacity to overcome his environment. He has lost the will to live and win. Of what practical value, then, is war?"

The reason most movements for peace in the past have failed is because they have had no practical plan of procedure. Gandhi realized that unorganized good-will cannot stand up against "disciplined violence" as he called war, and have a ghost of a chance of winning. So he set about organizing his peaceful army. He must meet organized brute force with organized soul force.

ORGANIZATION COUNTS

He must have officers for this army, trained in the essential weapons of self control and endurance under all provocation. To train such leaders Gandhi took young men and women . . . for women were as important passive resisters as men; when it came to endurance they were already past-masters of the art . . . into his new *Ashram* at Ahmedabad. It was in 1916 that he settled in Ahmedabad and established the *Ashram*. An *Ashram* is a community home—a place to seek the truth. He developed a library of many books. Regular classes were held, somewhat after the manner of the old Greek gymnasium school, with sociology, economics, politics and religion emphasized. There was an eight-fold vow that all students had to take.

First—truthfulness

Second—non-violence

Third—celibacy

Fourth—control of the palate

Fifth—non-stealing

Sixth—non possession

—that is, giving up all desire of possessing things.

Seventh—*Swadeshi*—that is, using home-grown, home-manufactured goods, and being loyal to one's own inherited culture, developing it from within, instead of becoming foreign.

Eighth—fearlessness

These young officers in the army of passive resistance then went out into all parts of the country, travelling third class, living on whatever small amounts the communities chose to give them, and taught the Indian villagers what *Satyagraha,* the pursuit of truth by non-violent measures, really meant. These Indian villages and the groups that gathered at universities and in cities were the training camps of the battalions of passive resistance. It was this training that made possible the battle of Bombay, and the successful boycott of British goods.

In August 1920 the non-cooperation movement was really launched on a national scale, with an appeal to every Indian to enter into this program as if this had been a war of arms instead of wills and of ideals. The will to Indian freedom was to be pushed forward by the force of truth. These new soldiers of passive resistance would not kill anyone to attain their end, but would allow themselves to be killed, if need be.

"We do not want to sacrifice the life of a single person to end British rule in India" said Gandhi. "But the Indians are willing that the holy Ganges should run red with blood (Indian blood) if this is necessary to gain them freedom so long unjustly delayed." This was the new fighting pacifism.

These were to be the weapons with which this new non-violent soldier would fight. The Indian Congress Manifesto of 1920 advised as means of non-cooperation the following definite things:

1. The surrender of all titles and honorary offices and resignation from nominated seats in the local government bodies.
2. Refusal to attend government receptions or levees, durbars, and other official and semi-official functions, held by government officials, or in their honor.
3. Gradual withdrawal of children from schools and colleges owned, aided or controlled by government, and in place of such schools and colleges, the establishment of national schools and colleges in the various provinces.
4. Gradual boycott of British courts by lawyers and litigants, and establishment of private arbitration courts by their aid for the settlement of private disputes.
5. Refusal on the part of the military, clerical, and laboring

classes to offer themselves as recruits for service in Mesopotamia or any other place.

6. Withdrawal by candidates of their candidature for election to the reformed councils, and refusal on the part of the voters to vote for any candidate who may, despite the Congress advice, offer himself for election.
7. The boycott of foreign goods, especially everything that is British-made.

The boycott of British goods was the "Big Bertha" of the passive resistance campaign; it all but stunned the British into defeat. Add to this, the refusal of the passive resisters to pay taxes, to hold office under the government, to keep British honors or souvenirs of war: in addition, pile up the women's surprisingly successful picketing of the liquor shops and of opium selling, where educated women of the leading families of India endured insults as they blocked the auction of government licenses. Here are weapons not to be despised.

Gandhi's defense of his use of this economic weapon was typically reasonable. He claimed that since the British government refused India the right to an autonomous government, either within or without the Empire, India had the right to set up an internal national policy of its own. "The boycott" said Gandhi "is merely India's tariff to protect her own native industries . . . as America for example, protects her manufacturies." The boycott then, was a tariff such as any country—France or America—might raise against another country in self-protection. The boycott method was made necessary because the Indians were given no legislative function.

But Gandhi did not stop there. To refuse to buy British cloth was not enough. India must herself develop her own industries so that she would not be dependent upon any foreign nation whatever. He got down the spinning wheel out of the Indian attics, at about the same time that our antique dealers were pulling American revolutionary spinning wheels out of the attics of New England. But the spinning wheel in India was no relic. It was a present need. And soon the very Himalayas began to echo back the whirr of patriotic Indian spinning. Here again Gandhi had vindicated his claim to being a practical idealist.

SOLDIERS IN HOMESPUN

The uniform for this new army of passive resisters was khaddar, native-woven Indian dress. First the spinning wheel, then the loin cloth. Gandhi identified himself with even the poorest of his people.

Gandhi's dress is not really just a loin cloth. The *dhoti* is actually more like our athletic trousers. The long loops of cloth draped around each leg come down below the knee. There is nothing incongruous about such a costume when the temperature is 120 degrees in the shade and often goes no lower all night than 100 degrees. The Indian homespun shawl for the market-place and the drawing room is like the Roman toga. It gives the Bengali gentleman a courtly dignity in the tropics.

Such a costume is certainly more appropriate for India than the trappings of the average European. No Londoner could have been more shocked at Gandhi's bare legs than is the Indian when he sees the European dress for the first time. He regards the European in India as a sort of vaudeville actor. When the temperature has soared away off the thermometer, he wears a white collar, and clothes that stay dry hardly long enough to get them on. Then he has to wear a strip of blanket down his spine and a helmet hat to keep from getting sunstroke. He eats meat on the hottest day; drinks whiskey till he looks as if he were going to burst a blood vessel. The Indian is first shocked . . . and then he sits back and laughs as at silly fools.

Gandhi wore European clothes during his London school days. When he put on his lawyer's frock coat, as a badge of office, he still wore his Indian turban. When he took the vow of identification with the suffering peasants of India, what was more natural than that he should adopt their own humble native costume? His *dhoti* is more than clothes; it is a symbol. A symbol to remind him daily that he is no longer a high-caste, but a peasant, fighting not for his own caste, but for all India.

On the recent trip to London it was not incongruous for him to retain his native costume. He was not at the London conference as an Englishman; . . . he was there as an Indian. His dress helped to remind him daily that he was an Indian patriot. He regarded partial nakedness as symbolical of the way England had stripped India.

It is chiefly because this return to Indian dress on the part of so many Indian intellectuals is symbolic, that the British oppose it so heartily . . . even to persecuting or repudiating an Indian official who wears the dress of his country. An Indian principal of a great college was told he must either cease wearing Indian clothes and go back to European, or the government would cancel the financial grant to the college of which he was president. Even foreign missionaries who have tried to adopt this comfortable dress of the country, suited to climatic needs, just as we expect foreigners in this country to adopt our American ways and dress (else why all our Americanization social work?) have been sent home by the British government. Thus "white prestige" is upheld, and the iron hand of government controls the educational policies, not only of English, but of Indian and foreign schools. Not only the educational policies, but the very pants the principal must wear! Is it any wonder that Gandhi refused to wear European clothes in London?

If dress had been the only way in which Gandhi identified himself with the peasant there might be just reason for criticism. But he has done much more.

A LABOR LEADER

In 1917 he began to take up the cause of industrial laborers, and wherever any difficulty broke out he would nearly always be the first on the scene. For instance, in 1917, when the working conditions of the Indian laborers on the indigo plantations of Bengal brought about difficulties, Gandhi went directly to that region and settled down to try to solve the problems by the use of his Satyagraha philosophy. Warrants were served upon him and he was asked by government to leave the district. He disobeyed the order and was brought to court. He was not sent to jail at this time. The government even appointed him a member of a commission to try to bring about a permanent settlement of the agrarian difficulties.

In many similar movements among the peasants, miners and industrial workers Gandhi moved back and forth across the whole of India, weaving the millions of the populace into a solid phalanx of loyalty to Indian ideals, and opposition to foreign control and domination. He became the idol of the common people.

More than once has he personally reminded me that his task was one of reconciliation. Even after the tragedy in the bloody garden at Amritsar, when thousands of unarmed Indians had been shot down, the National Congress of India, under Gandhi's insistence, had made this their aim—"The attainment of self-government within the British Empire by the people of India by all legal, constitutional, and non-violent means."

Just because a few Englishmen, like General Dyer, of the old school, believe the Orient understands nothing but armed tyranny, it must not be concluded that justice does not remain under the English Crown, argued Gandhi. This was an individual, not a national policy, he insisted . . . and in thus insisting, he probably saved the lives of thousands of British residents in India.

The Indian National Congress, of which Gandhi is the chief, yet not the only power, is the real governing force in India today, so far as Indian loyalties go. It is not recognized by British authorities any more than the American Continental Congress was recognized by King George the Third. It meets whenever and wherever it can. It had been clamoring for some time for early freedom within or without the British Empire; and in 1920, disenchanted and disillusioned by the government use of the Rowlatt Act, (the same government which had promised India "self-determination" during the war) Gandhi agreed to the demands of the Congress. From then on the goal of passive resistance should be "the attainment of self-government by the people of India by all legitimate and peaceful means."

Still Gandhi held himself above retaliation; he did not want revenge upon England; he wanted only justice, freedom. This attitude nearly cost him his life more than once at the hands of radical Indian patriots.

Two Indians had killed an English official in the Punjab, and Gandhi had been asked to try to save the lives of these young men who had been condemned to death. Gandhi refused. "I cannot condone the killing of anyone," he said. The furious friends of the condemned men came rushing one day into Gandhi's quiet room to kill him also, as no patriot, since he would not intercede to save his fellow Indians.

As those big warriors stood over him, Gandhi looked at them unafraid.

"You may take my life if you wish . . ." he said quietly. "It is all I have left. I have no property I can give you. All I have is love. . . . I'd give everything I have to help you, but I cannot. If I led our people to violence to avenge this political murder, I would be using the very methods of force I deplore. Kill me if you like . . . but I must stick to my truth. Love is stronger than death."

They did not kill him; they knelt and kissed his feet. And passive resistance had won another dramatic battle.

Incidents like this have served to lift Gandhi's power, not only among the thinking Indians but among the English themselves. It is a strange contradiction in terms for a man to be the friend of the very people he is fighting. Yet Gandhi's power lies just there. He refuses to hate, to take an unfair advantage of anyone . . . even his enemy. How can you attack a man like that? How conquer him?

JAILS BECOME HOTELS

The only thing that government could do to such passive resisters was to put them in jail. And this it did with such vim and vigor that now about twenty-seven thousand political prisoners are thus boarded by the government. But going to jail in such good company soon lost its opprobrium. It became quite the thing socially in India to go to jail just as the depression has brought American women to the proud use of their last year's hats! Not that jail life was easy. Most of the rooms where the prisoners are kept are over-crowded, poorly ventilated and the prisoners have difficulty in getting the diet to which they are accustomed. In addition, the sentences of hard labor which many of these political prisoners draw, means back-breaking labor on streets, railroads, and other physical exertion on the part of scholars and professional men who have never before carried anything heavier than a pen or a pocketbook. Even the women, used to silken luxury, are forced to wash and clean till some of them literally drop, fainting with fatigue. But the Indian spirit remains unbroken, because the jail no longer means disgrace; it is almost a disgrace today for a patriotic Indian to be out of jail.

Even the children of India know this.

"The same mistake that Germany made when she executed Edith Cavell, a British magistrate made in Bombay last week" remarks a leading periodical recently.

"Outside a Bombay store a small, impertinent boy shrilly shouted to purchasers to buy nothing but Indian goods. Policemen swooped down, arrested the child as a picketer, and hauled him off to court where a short tempered magistrate sentenced him to four years imprisonment. The child's name was Krishna Kant. He was nine years old. Snapped the magistrate: 'If you disobey orders in the reformatory you will be whipped.'

"'I am ready to die for Gandhi' said Krishna Kant.

"The next day all India knew of Krishna Kant."

This story is strangely reminiscent of the remark of General Howe in Boston, during the American Revolution, when a group of indignant school boys came to him to protest that the British soldiers were spoiling the coasting upon Boston Common. "How can you expect to conquer a people" asked General Howe, "when the very school boys breathe independence?"[1]

Gandhi in jail, also, proved to be as powerful, if not more so, than when free. His peaceful army was so well organized that it could march on without him. That is the power of

---

[1] Michigan *Christian Advocate*, 1932.

Gandhi's non-violent methods . . . the soul goes marching on. This soul power, or emotionalism, if you choose to call it so, has always been the moving force behind armies, whether with or without guns. Most people do not live in their intellects, they live in their emotions: love of child, husband, father, mother, country. That is why the first thing set up at the beginning of a new war is the propaganda office. This surge of idealism, of emotions, whatever you wish, is the imponderable which has made and unmade empires.

The passive resistance movement has cost the British government more in time, worry, and actual cash than any other uprising within the empire since the time of the American Revolution. Since Gandhi was put in jail in 1932 not a yard of British cloth has been sold in the Bombay bazaars . . . this from news reports released by government agencies. There is small market for government licenses for liquor saloons due to the successful non-violent picketing of Indian women. The hunger in the streets of Lancashire is but the echo of the stern boycott of British goods by the Gandhi followers. Is this a fanatical or a practical war? This war with the guns of will and the spirit.

Not a rifle or machine gun has been fired by a Gandhi follower. There have been sporadic violent uprisings, brought about by rebel objectors to passive resistance. But last year, according to government figures, only a few hundred people out of the three hundred and fifty million Indians and the one hundred and fifty thousand Europeans in India, were killed by these uprisings—less than were killed and crippled through automobile accidents in Detroit last year. The will to peace can be organized, as the will to force is organized.

As the *Journal des Nations* commented upon Gandhi's recent visit to Geneva:

"Here is a mystic, but a mystic who has been able to hold

his own against great statesmen. Non-violence is not only a mystic creed as it was for Tolstoy; it is equally a political force which has met with remarkable success. Gandhi's message has two aspects, just as he has two faces. His ascetic features are lightened up by a very knowing smile, such as one sees on the portraits of old diplomatic cardinals. He is a stranger, whose thoughts we Europeans cannot unravel. Let Great Britain beware, if she does not solve this riddle."

CHAPTER V

AMERICAN INFLUENCES

ON THAT balmy night, not so long ago, when Gandhi was arrested and taken from his bed on the roof of a Bombay house, it was discovered that he had on the table at his bed-side a copy of Henry Thoreau's essay on Civil Disobedience. He took this book with him to prison, together with his few articles of clothing, and his spinning wheel. A curious friend-ship this, of ancient India for young America, still in its national swaddling clothes in the family of the ages! Yet the Indian peaceful revolution has taken many of its weapons from the minds and lips of Americans. In a very real sense the seeds of Indian revolution were planted in America.

"Under a government which imprisons any unjustly, the true place for a just man is also a prison," Thoreau tells this Indian patriot again on his way to jail. "The only proper place which Massachusetts has provided for her freer, less desponding spirits is in her prisons, to be put out and locked out of the State by her own act, as they have already put themselves out by their own principles."[1] Thoreau is, of course, writing of the American fugitive slave act which provided that any captured slave had to be returned to his white master, during those days, eighty years ago, when the North and South were violently disagreeing about slavery in Amer-

---

[1] Thoreau, Henry D., Essay on *Civil Disobedience*. Pages 370, 371.

ica, and when even brothers quarreled, and home after home was divided against itself.

"If the alternative is to keep all just men in prison, or to give up war and slavery, the State will not hesitate which to choose" goes on Thoreau. Then he gives Gandhi a practical hint. "If a thousand men were not to pay their tax bills this year, that would not be as violent and bloody a measure as it would be to pay them, and enable the State to commit violence and shed innocent blood. This, in fact, is a peaceful revolution, if any such is possible." This is exactly what Gandhi and the Indian Congress have advised the passive resisters to do; to refuse to pay taxes . . . which means prison and confiscation of property for them.

But Gandhi goes still farther along the path with Thoreau. "If the tax gatherer or any other public officer asks me, as one has done, 'But what shall *I* do?' My answer is, 'If you really wish to do anything, resign your office.' When the subject has refused allegiance, and the officer has resigned his office, then the revolution is accomplished." (Thoreau.)

Here again India has followed America's advice; one of the chief embarrassments of the British government in India today is that many of her trained Indian servants have refused longer to hold office, even though, by so doing, they cut off their own incomes.

This is a new India, an almost unbelievable India, which is thus declaring its right to independent action. When I first came to India in 1904 it was a patient, easy-going, tropical country, slumbering peacefully under the mango trees at noon, careless of who ruled it, accepting suffering as its right . . . even enjoying it. For it is only by a mortification of the flesh, teach the old Indian sages, that the spirit can grow or be free.

As Matthew Arnold describes it,

"The East bowed low before the blast
In silent, deep disdain
She let the legions thunder past
And plunged in thought again." [1]

When stocks were sold on the London exchange to raise money to build the first Indian railroad, London was afraid to buy because of possible Indian uprisings. But one of the chief engineers quieted these fears by writing home,

"Don't worry. These Indians will never rise. I build the railway by dragging trees from the jungle to cut into ties. I could go to the villages and drag out humans, strapping them to the rails and running the engine over them, without a neighbor or a relative rising up to avenge their death. Life means nothing to them. They cannot be stirred." This was the old India.

When I first met Gandhi in 1917 I realized a new India had been born. The war was on that Christmas time so I could not get passage from Marseilles to Bombay. Every inch of space was used for soldiers and supplies. I finally had to go round by Japan and China, though even there the jaunty *Emden* chased us most of the way. But, certainly, I thought, the war cannot have touched India deeply; she is too vast, too wrapped up in her own concerns of living, suffering, dying. But as soon as I came near the port of Colombo, Ceylon, the excitement of the new India came out to greet me. In the old days there had been nothing more thrilling in Ceylon than bananas growing on trees; the smell of spices; quiet priestly monasteries; mildly solicitous shopkeepers; the soft pad of languid Indian feet in the streets. But here was a new Ceylon! Here were excited crowds, swarming the port, the streets, the very housetops.

[1] Arnold, Matthew, in *Matthew Arnold's Poems*. (New York, 1883.) Page 301.

I wanted to study this change of front, to learn the secret of this newly vibrant people, so I got off the boat and took the train and ferry a six day's journey up through Madras, the great City of the South, to Calcutta on the north east, and finally to Delhi. I found everywhere a new pulsing, nationally-conscious India. People who used languidly to discuss Rama were talking politics; on every side you heard them arguing about the steel workers, home industries, home rule.

WOODROW WILSON

I saw for the first time in Indian homes pictures of American Statesmen—Lincoln, Roosevelt, Washington; and heard the name of Woodrow Wilson upon the streets of Indian cities. India had formerly been so dominated by Europe that America had been merely a far-off unreal dream. But this new political idealism had bridged the seas of centuries and I heard the words, "self-determination for all nations" on educated Indian lips everywhere. But there was another name that I heard more often. "Gandhi says . . ." said the man who drove my carriage. "Gandhi thinks . . ." murmured the bank clerk where I cashed my checks. Gandhi everywhere. Not as Mahatma Gandhi, a saint, but as a political idealist like Wilson. Who was this Gandhi? Knowing India, I could not conceive how any living person, who had not yet become a dead saint, could be on every tongue. I decided I must see this man; and I did.

Any one who is not prepared to capitulate to Gandhi had better stay away from him. The power of his personality, the fire in his great brown eyes, his innate dignity, draw you, irresistibly. You forget yourself; you forget Gandhi as a man. His deep voice carries to you his message only. It is because he has sunk himself so deeply in his ideal, that he has lost all self-consciousness; and therefore is greater than his puny body. I have known men to say, "I hate him. I despise everything for which he stands!" And then I have greeted them as they came away from Gandhi, murmuring, "I was mistaken!" Love him, or hate him, if you can . . . you cannot ignore him. He remains unique.

"I haven't known much about America," Gandhi said to me as I sat down beside him. "I had been taught by my English friends to believe that the United States is not a real democracy. But Woodrow Wilson sounds like a true democrat and a great statesman. He fascinates us Indians. While I have been supporting the British Empire in this war to end war, I have admired Wilson for being 'too proud to fight'. My very principles of life call out to him . . . for I too do not believe in taking human life; any life. But now that he has brought you into the war, perhaps we are not all wrong."

Gandhi later changed his mind . . . as Wilson might have done had he lived to see our modern chaos. Gandhi decided that war as a means of settling international disputes was useless. The only thing that could bring peace was an insistence upon peaceful methods. We must organize for peace as we had for war, every man, woman and child; we must build up a public opinion for passive resistance so strong that machine guns could not shatter it. India had gone a step farther, but the influence of American ideals remained in the Gandhi movement.

America for the past century and a half of her existence has had continually an upsetting influence upon the older and more settled civilizations. Our American Revolution may have had little to do with the actual upheaval of French society, but at least the success of the American principle of "no taxation without representation" gave added impetus to the French

Revolution. Our dramatic Civil War made slavery the subject of world-wide discussion, and brought slave-holding anywhere into disrepute. It was Thoreau's reaction to slavery that caused him to coin an entirely new term, "Civil Disobedience" . . . which was later to become the watchword of the Indian Revolution of today.

THOREAU

Gandhi had first got hold of Thoreau while a law student in London; and the writings of Thoreau introduced him to Emerson. It is curious that both these American protestants against slavery should have been students of Hindu culture.

In 1862 when Thoreau died he left his library of Hindu literature to Emerson, and from that time forward Emerson seems to have bathed himself in eastern philosophies, and to have appreciated them perhaps more than any American up to this time. He writes in one of his journals, "The East is grand and makes Europe appear the land of trifles." And again we find, "In the sleep of great heats there was nothing for me but to read the Vedas, the Bible of the tropics, which I find I come back upon every three or four years. It is sublime as heat and night and breathless ocean . . . it is of no use to put away the book. If I trust myself in the woods . . . nature makes a Brahman of me presently: eternal necessity, eternal compensation, unfathomable power, unbroken silence—this is her creed."

EMERSON

Emerson must have loved the Bhagavad Gita and Vishnu Puranas almost as much as Gandhi does today. Indeed Emerson's "Brahma" is but a poetical rendering of a passage from the Gita.

"If the red slayer thinks he slays,
Or if the slain thinks he is slain,

They know not well the subtle ways
  I keep, and pass, and turn again.

Far or forgot to me is near;
  Shadow and sunlight are the same;
The vanished gods to me appear;
  And one to me are shame and fame.

They reckon ill who leave me out;
  When me they fly, I am the wings;
I am the doubter and the doubt,
  And I the hymn the Brahman sings.

The strong gods pine for my abode,
  And pine in vain the sacred Seven;
But thou, meek lover of the good!
  Find me, and turn thy back on heaven."

Frederic Ives Carpenter[1] says that this is not only one of Emerson's best poems, but is one of the finest expressions of the Hindu idea of absolute unity.

Little did Emerson think that a generation later an Indian boy in London would sniff at human slavery and exclaim again, "There is infamy in the air!" This time the slavery was in India, not America: but it was still the oppressive policy of the white man against another race.

If by revolutionary is meant a belief in the inherent right of every human being to freedom of life and conscience, then the American missionary has been also a revolutionary element in India. He did not aggressively preach democracy, but by his very way of thinking and living, by his freedom from forms and conventions, he brought a peculiar emphasis to the Orient. France, Germany, Switzerland, and England, have brought their own national contributions to the east.

---

[1] Carpenter, Frederic Ives, *Emerson and Asia*, Harvard University Press.

DEMOCRACY

The American's innate democracy made him go straight to the downtrodden masses of India, to the "untouchables". Coming from a civilization where even the laborers had a right to sanitation, education, hygiene, leisure, the heart of many an American missionary was stirred as much or more by the physical and social degradation of the untouchables as by their spiritual poverty. Christianity has always expressed itself in social reform. The American missionary did not mean to strike at the imperial government of India, at the country's social structure as such, at the prosperity of the great industrial concerns. He was appalled to the depths of his democratic soul by the slavery of a people who could not drink at the common wells but must push aside the scum from wayside streams; who could not shop at grocery stores but had to shriek their wants from a safe distance and then go and pick up what the store keeper chose to give them; who could not even walk upon the same roads as the Brahmans, but who must slink to their destination by roundabout paths; whose very shadow was unclean.

Schools and churches were snatched at eagerly by these depressed classes and outcastes who had nothing to lose and everything to gain. The natural result was a mass movement towards organized Christianity which promised the untouchable his first social relief in centuries; whole villages begged to be instructed and to be baptized into the church where each man was as good as another and where all men were brothers. That this should arouse antagonism among certain European groups and among high caste Hindus was inevitable. Not that the Europeans did not have their own missionaries among the untouchables, but somehow this wholesale democratic enthusiasm of the Americans seemed, what shall I say? somewhat precipitate.

WILLIAM LLOYD GARRISON

It was only, however, when the leaders among the Hindus themselves took up the relief of the untouchables that the question as to whether or not these fifty millions of people would ever be raised to social and political equality in India was settled. When Gandhi sent out his stinging indictment of untouchability as slavery; when high caste Brahmans, Gandhi's adherents, stood for nearly a year, sometimes almost shoulder deep in water, upon a road from which the untouchables had been excluded, and thereby won the freedom of the way for all; when a Brahman flung across the front of his weekly paper "The Indian Social Reformer" the words of William Lloyd Garrison, the American abolitionist,

> "I will be as harsh as truth, and as uncompromising as justice; I am in earnest . . . I will not equivocate . . . I will not excuse . . . I will not retreat a single inch . . . and I will be heard."

When such men as these came out against untouchability, child marriage, purdah, then, and then only was social reform assured in India. It was in a revealing conversation with Gandhi that I first got a clear idea of Indian social reforms apart from my own religion and race. He asked me to demonstrate with any sort of logic the claim that we Christian missionaries, or government officials, foreigners at best, could accomplish any more in this field than sincere Hindu idealists and reconstructionists. He wanted to know if God or the spirit of Christ could not inspire and work through them as well as through us? His question carried its own answer.

The English government desired social reform in India, if it could be secured without political and commercial disturbances; but they wished to develop this reform in their own way. The direct American way of doing things always seemed to please the Indians, but to run counter to English methods and wishes. The American tradition of free public schools for all the people, for example, was in contradiction to the English tradition both at home and in India. The English theory of education is that the government is not primarily responsible for the education of its youth above the early grades, so that if the parent wants his child to have a fairly complete instruction, he has to send him to some private school founded by an individual, sect, or community. This is the official policy in India. Mohammedans, Hindus, Christians, must establish their own schools. This emphasizes differences and increases disunity among these elements of Indian life. Government backing and funds have been given to such of these schools as stick to the English standards and loyalties, but all too often when a school shows the slightest sign of becoming *Indian* instead of predominantly Mohammedan, Hindu, or Christian, or of giving to the Indian children the wealth of their own background and culture, the government support is decreased or withdrawn. Thus the old principle of "divide and rule" runs down through even the educational system.

But it is not so much the content of American teaching, but the very attitude of equality with the Indian, that antagonizes government agents. The missionary from Boston and Indianapolis went to India to get close to the Indian and to share with him his ideals; therefore, he saw no incongruity in going to Indian homes and in having Indians, without regard to creed or caste, in his home as guests. He had no "white prestige" in his inner consciousness, and for that very reason did more to raise the white man in the brown man's estimation than if he had consciously set out to accomplish this end.

AN ALIEN COMPLEX

The American missionary, especially the modern youngster, has usually no objection to adopting Indian dress; which is cool, comfortable, and in keeping with the surrounding atmosphere. It is natural, also for an American teacher to walk through an Indian class room, to lay his hand on a student's shoulder, to smile at him with a camaraderie impossible if the foreign teacher is endued with the ruler's complex of the exaggerated respect due a white man. The American came on a purely friendly mission; he had no axe to grind; no imperial policy to uphold. Both of these attitudes, English and American, are largely unconscious and inherited; but they have their effect, nevertheless, upon the Indian mind. Thus, not only is the bond between democratic America and the freedom-thirsty Indian cemented, but the fissure of suspicion between the American missionary and the British government widens. The upshot of it is that many Americans become more British than the British, while others are crowded out and return home rather than surrender their ideals.

The average young American who goes out to India dreams of serving the outcaste, of bringing hygiene and medicine to the masses, of becoming a friend to Indians. He does not understand that he is going to Imperial Britain, where every lecture he makes, every class he conducts, in literature, religion, manual training, farming, is supervised and limited by British ideas. And being unused to surveillance, it not unnaturally irritates the American to be treated as a suspicious alien. He knows that millions of American dollars and hundreds of American lives have gone into Christian churches in India to help the country, and he chafes under the suspicion that he might wish to nudge Great Britain out as a ruler, and to plant the American flag on Indian soil.

The policy of the government can be interpreted as discriminating against American missions. The American missionary went to India to cooperate, not to supplant. Seeing no need of duplication of effort, he established his mission college, in many cases, near the government university in order that there might be an exchange of classes such as goes on between nearby colleges everywhere, as for instance, Barnard and Columbia, or Radcliffe and Harvard. But suddenly a law was passed by the government a few years ago, providing that no college within a certain number of miles of a government university could carry students up to graduation, the final instruction to be by government staff only. This ruling was supposed to apply to all colleges. But it is a curious fact that certain British colleges and other sect institutions affected by the law, have found some loophole to wiggle through and have secured satisfactory adjustments. Not a single American college has been able to regain its lost privileges. Thus at one sweep American colleges near certain government universities are degraded, reduced to the status of junior colleges or high schools; discriminated against without redress.

It is almost too bad to stop with a solitary illustration of this kind because scores of specific cases in all departments of life could be cited. The one instance simply indicates the nervous fear and the calculated scheme of protection caused by what an alien government calls the alien activities of other friendly nationalities. It would seem that the naïve Americans have planted unintentionally effective seeds of new life.

An English missionary recently announced, unscathed, "We are in the year two of the Gandhi Era!" An American, making such a remark, would find himself slated for the first boat home. Why? Just because the seeds that America and England have been sowing are different.

The Gandhi movement is impregnated with American ideals; with Thoreau, Emerson, Wilson, Lincoln. Answering the claim that Britain is in India for India's own good, and that India is not fit to rule herself, the literature of the movement quotes the words of Abraham Lincoln:

> "In all ages of the world, tyrants have justified themselves in conquering and enslaving peoples by declaring that they were doing it for their own benefit. Turn it whatever way you will, whether it comes from the mouth of a king, or from the mouth of the men of one race as a reason for enslaving the men of another race, it is the same old serpent. They all say that they bestride the necks of the people not because they want to do this, but because the people are so much better off for being ridden. You work and I eat. You toil and I will enjoy the fruits of your toil. The argument is the same and the bondage is the same." . . . "Any people anywhere, being inclined and having the power, have the right to rise up and shake off an existing government which they deem unjust and tyrannical and form a new one which suits them better. This is a most valuable, a most sacred right, a right we hope and believe will liberate the world."

Plant such seeds in the west and you have great united democracies; scatter them in the fierce tropics, and you have . . . Gandhi. American sympathy for India has never been organized. But the literature of freedom has brought inspiration, and the friendship of individuals has cheered the leaders. Lajpat Rai dedicates his book, "Unhappy India"

> "With love and gratitude to those numberless American men and women who stand for the freedom of the world; who know no distinction of colour, race, or creed; and who profess a religion of love, humanity and justice. To them the oppressed people of the earth look for sympathy in their struggle for emancipation, and in them is centred the hope of world peace."

CHAPTER VI

CAN A HINDU BE A CHRISTIAN?

GANDHI is a Hindu. He says so. All India knows it. Yet he lives the Sermon on the Mount. Is he also a Christian?

This is an age of scientific testing, even of religion. Christianity, along with all other philosophies of living, must meet the modern test of utility. Will it work . . . every day? That is what the young Christians and Hindus the world over are asking of Christianity and Hinduism, respectively. What makes a Christian different from any other man? Modern youth knows little and cares less about theology; whether a man was sprinkled or dipped by a licensed priest of any given sect of the Christian church. The two-fold simple question is: What does he do? What is he?

Our era, with its huge belief in its modernity, is measuring once again by the same yardstick that Christ used,

"By their fruits you shall know them."

The principles, the man himself; the life; the character. Jesus did not say to the Roman executioner, at the foot of the cross, when the thief on the other cross asked for forgiveness, "Permit me to come down to baptize this man." The thief did not subscribe to any creed but Christ. Yet the greatest authority on Christianity that the world will ever know said to the thief, "This day shalt thou be with me in Paradise."

Measured by this yardstick, there are thousands of Hindus in India today who are Christians. Over and over again men have come to me in Hindu temples to say that they were trying to guide their lives by the principles of Christ. Yet they were not listed in any statistics of Christian church membership . . . and never will be.

I have walked through the aisles of class rooms in a Hindu university and found students poring over the New Testament. I have picked up the New Testament in Hindu libraries and found notations on the margins . . . which is more than I have found in many European and American libraries. This is a curious fact, considering our western practise of passing out graduates from our universities without their even "cracking" a Bible. Yet in a native state, whose state religion is Hinduism, and where the Maharajah, a Hindu, supports the educational system, there is a university where no student can get his degree of bachelor of arts or science until he has mastered the New Testament as well as his chemistry text book.

TOUCHING THE UNTOUCHABLES

Not long ago, in the town where a Hindu college professor lives, an outcaste had fallen dead on the streets. Orthodox caste men who saw this body ran away from it. But this Brahman walked over to the body and saw there a fellow Indian. He went to some of his caste friends—lawyers, professors, business men, and said, "Let us prove that we are worthy of the name of Brahman. Let us show that caste is broken down here in our town." Seven Brahman friends joined him. They lifted the body of the outcaste, laid it on a stretcher and, acting as bearers, carried it to the bank of the river. Here they brought pieces of wood to make a funeral pyre and burned the body, giving this outcaste a full Hindu burial, scattering the ashes on the river. Thus was the brotherhood of man illustrated practically in this town of New India.

Was this college professor a Christian? He was not a member of any Christian church. He had come to me one day after watching our ceremony where, as Bishop, I ordained a number of young ministers. He said,

"I believe that the ideals of your Christ are what India needs. I wish you would ordain me too!"

I looked up at him; regal, towering above me, in his flowing Bengali shawl.

"But I cannot ordain you. You're not a Christian!"

"I am not baptized," he admitted. "Nor do I want to be . . . I want only to live out the Christ principles in my town. Can you not, though, send me out as a social servant of Jesus Christ?"

To want to live Christ . . . was this not the full measure of Christianity? Is every Roman Catholic who has been baptized, whether he is a gangster or a social worker, a Christian? Is every Protestant whether he thieves on the high road at night or by day in the bucket shop, a Christian?

I gave this Hindu my hand. We had a consecration service at a Christian altar where I placed my hands reverently upon his head; and he went forth "a social servant of Jesus Christ."

What did he do? As editor of an important newspaper, he began reforms which only his great influence and high standing in the community made it possible for him to put across. His editorials, flowing through Hindu life as no baptized Christian's ever could, came out against untouchability, caste, illiteracy, all forms of religious bigotry and social injustice. He attacked liquor as demoralizing the youth of India. He came out firmly against the government selling opium as it does postage stamps. Gambling and prostitution had been the two great evils of the annual *mela* (festival), which to the Hindu means a sort of combination of our country fair and an old fashioned camp meeting. People thronged by the thousands to see *Yogi* priests bury themselves in sand and yet miraculously breathe. Pilgrims came for a bath in the holy river. Food, music, entertainments, shows, abounded . . . including those of the nautch girls and of the gamblers. The Brahman-Christian editor not only used his newspaper to arouse public opinion to banish prostitution and gambling, but inaugurated the provision of a better milk supply for babies, and social hygiene.

KARMA

It is in the building of character that Christianity is important to both east and west. From this point of view, it is interesting to discover how many attitudes of mind Christianity and Hinduism have in common. Is predestination, the idea that God selects the people he is going to save before they are born, so different from the Hindu law of *Karma?* *Karma* is the scientific doctrine of evolution applied to human lives throughout the aeons of immortality; that is, that man in the next life will reap what he sows in this. If a man follows the rules of Hinduism and of his caste he advances towards the highest caste, the Brahman. If he is not true to his ideals, he may be born a mouse . . . or a louse. However, his eventual destiny is to raise his spiritual standard through each incarnation till at last he is at one with the Mind that created the Universe. Many Christians have a similar belief; that a bad man goes to purgatory, from which he may be helped out by prayers until he attains heaven.

How do we know that the doctrine of reincarnation, of gradual advance to perfection, is false? Science believes that energy cannot be destroyed; the form may change, but the energy itself goes on. The Hindu applies this spiritually. The Christian with his belief in immortality, still does not know where his friends are who have died. "The golden streets" that the saints walk may not necessarily be so much metal; "golden" may simply be an oriental picture of a place of exquisite beauty. The important thing in both the Hindu and Christian philosophies is the feature they have in common, namely, that a man reaps what he sows in this life and the next.

AHIMSA

In the doctrine of *Ahimsa,* doing no harm to any living creature, upon which Gandhi has based his program of passive resistance, lies one of the chief similarities between Hinduism and Christianity. It may be that Christian philosophy even borrowed this idea from early Hindu or Buddhist thought.

It is altogether possible that Jesus was influenced by *Ahimsa.* Just before the birth of Christ, Buddhism had spread over the world—not only throughout India, China, Japan, Korea, Siam and Tibet, but in Asia Minor itself. There were rumors that Jesus himself came to India in his young manhood, though the books written in favor of this thesis seem to be without historical foundation. *Ahimsa* is older even than Buddha. But Buddha sucked out of Hindu thought the most regnant doctrines of his religion. He was a Hindu, as Jesus was a Jew, by birth and training. It is no careless leap of imagination to say that it may have been the doctrine of *Ahimsa* that gave Jesus the Sermon on the Mount. It takes nothing away from the timeless significance of his life and of his message to say that he was sufficiently educated and experienced in world thought as to have drunk at the fountain of Indian wisdom, literature.

Be this as it may, both the Hindu Gita and the Christian New Testament proclaim this theory of doing no harm, and of redemption through vicarious love.

GITA

The Bhagavad Gita, or The Song of God, is that portion of the Mahabharata, the Bible of Hinduism, which is most read by educated Hindus, especially those trained in modern Indian universities. The Gita has often been compared to the Gospel of St. John, and is about the same length. The Gita portrays a living God of love, who "brings himself to bodied earth" . . . that is, here is found the doctrine of the incarnation of God in man. Animal sacrifice has been given up for a sacrifice of the spirit. When the Gita was written it was heresy to the orthodox Hindus; it is now the very cream of orothdoxy. Just as the views of Christ were violently opposed to those of the Pharisees, and are now the norm of Christian spiritual life.

Most Hindu thought, outside the Gita, advises flight from the world, but the Gita advises all men to work in the world; and this philosophy of service explains not only its appeal to Gandhi but its great popularity with the modern educated youth of India.

A comparison of the teachings of the Gita and of the New Testament reveals them as startlingly similar at certain points.

The New Testament:

> "Not every one that saith unto me, Lord, Lord, shall enter into the Kingdom of Heaven, but he that doeth the will of my Father which is in Heaven."

The Gita:

> "He who does my work, who is given over to Me, who is devoted to Me . . . comes to Me."

Would not a life like Gandhi's, based on self-forgetfulness, poverty, temperance, devotion to a great ideal, be much the

© Keystone-Underwood

GANDHI AND ONE OF HIS YOUNGER ENTHUSIASTS

same whether it was based upon either of the following principles—

The Gita:

> "Holding in indifference alike pleasure and pain, gain and loss, conquest and defeat, so make thyself ready for the fight.

The New Testament:

> "Take no thought for your life, what ye shall eat or what ye shall drink; nor yet for your body, what ye shall put on. Is not the life more than meat and the body than raiment?"

The New Testament:

> "Love your enemies . . . do good to them that despitefully use you."
> "Whosoever shall smite thee on thy right cheek, turn to him the other also."

The Gita:

> "These though they smite me I would not smite, even for the sake of empire." "Verily it were better to eat even the food of beggary without slaughter."

Surely, concluded Gandhi, comparing these two sources when he was a student in London, there can be small distinction between the best Hinduism as represented in the Gita and the New Testament revelation through Christ. Both must be from the same great source. And upon this rock he has built not only his life but his political platform. Many people are willing to stake their chances in a possible hereafter upon a theory; but not so many of them are willing to build this same theory into their program of politics. They are willing to take a chance upon a hypothetical tomorrow, but not upon a sure today.

WAS WHITTIER A HINDU?

But this Hindu is not the only student to discover that Christianity and Hinduism, the Gospels and the Gita, have much in common. John Greenleaf Whittier, our Quaker poet, who like Thoreau and Emerson caught inspiration from the sacred books of Hinduism, has put many of the essentially similar doctrines into beautiful verse.

The following, entitled "Conduct" is from the Mahabharata,

"Heed how thou livest!
Do not act by day
Which from the night shall
Drive thy peace away.
In months of sun
So live that months of rain
Shall still be happy,
Evermore restrain evil
And cherish good
So shall there be
Another and a happier
Life for thee."[1]

Note also this Quaker rendering of "The Inward Judge" from the "Institutes of Manu"

"The soul itself its awful witness is:
Say not in evil doing 'No one sees'
And so offend the conscious one within
Whose ear can hear the silences of sin
Ere they find voice,
Whose eyes, unsleeping, see

[1] The poetical works of John Greenleaf Whittier, Frederick Warne & Co., London, page 551.

The secret motives of iniquity;
Nor in thy folly say 'I am alone'
For seated in thy heart, as on a throne,
The ancient judge and witness liveth still
To note thy act and thought
And as thy ill or good goes from thee,
Far beyond thy reach,
The solemn Doomsman's seal is set on each." [1]

There is an ethical story from the ancient Vedas written in Sanskrit, of how a wicked king tries to persuade his hunchback satellite to commit murder for him, by assuring him that there would be no one to witness the deed. The hunchback sets forth to do the bidding of the king, as he has always done unquestioningly before, but an inner voice stops him. He hastens back and cries, that he cannot kill:

"All nature would behold the crime
The spirits of the grove, the sun, the moon,
The winds, the vault of heaven
The firm-set earth,
Yama, the mighty god of all who die
Aye, and the inner conscience of my soul."

The great Christian social doctrine is the re-making of human society upon the basis of the Christ ideals. This is precisely what Gandhi is trying to do. Yet a western Christian civilization calls him "mystical" "impractical" and finds him impossible to understand.

G. K. Chesterton, admittedly a devout churchman, remarks,

"Modern Englishmen do not fight Gandhi because they have no notion of where in heaven or earth or under the

[1] The poetical works of John Greenleaf Whittier, Frederick Warne & Co., London, page 550.

earth his soul is really to be found. There is no agreement about terms or tests or the nature of truth."[1]

Perhaps if more of us studied the Sermon on the Mount as seriously as Gandhi does, we would understand him better. Even today, after nearly forty years of testing the practical wisdom of its precepts, Gandhi urges the young men of India, to "drink deep at this fountain."

The difficulty here is that it is almost impossible for the westerner to dissociate Christ from western civilization. The Indian does this easily. He reads the New Testament as he would his oriental scriptures, for the Bible is an oriental book. The Indian gets its significance immediately. He does not require an explanation in great detail.

"In my Father's house are many mansions."'

The Hindu knows that when he was married there was a small apartment added to his father's house to make ready for the new family, and that more rooms were added till there were enough for all the sons.

> "Lay not up for yourselves treasures upon earth, where moth and rust doth corrupt, and where thieves break through and steal."

is an oriental picture. The Indian thinks not only of the very rich who have their great treasure rooms into which they go to actually touch their bars of gold, the top layers of their buckets of pearls and rubies; but he knows that even in his own village when his father has had any money, he has dug a hole in the earth and stored his treasure. He understands therefore, that

[1] New York *Times*, Feb. 21, 1932.

"Where your treasure is, there will your heart be also."
"If you bring your gift to the altar . . ."

brings the picture of the altar of the Hindu temple, where he is accustomed to take his offerings. Again he reads,

"Whosoever shall compel thee to go a mile, go with him twain . . ."

This is not an allegory to him. It is a reality. Does he not walk sometimes five miles back and forth to the field from his little village, and does he not often meet a wayfarer by the way?

BAPTISM AND STIFF COLLARS

Many Hindus, understanding and approving Christian doctrines, do not become baptized Christians because this means giving up their families, their social position, and their influence in the community. Not that adopting the essential doctrines of Christ necessarily means this; it is because Christianity as presented to them is a system of western civilization which demands precedence over Indian social customs. "Adopt 'my' way of living, of thinking, of dressing!" demands the westerner. But may not the oriental interpretation of the Christian message be as accurate as the Anglo-Saxon or the Latin? Is Christianity a matter of wearing tweed pants and a stiff collar? Of drinking goat's milk or coffee? Of whiskey and soda?

The adoption of Christ's ideals may change many of the Hindu social customs, as for instance, when Gandhi began to pattern his life after the Sermon on the Mount. But to adopt Christ's ideals would equally change our manner of western living . . . if we really practised them.

Gandhi received from his mother his first lesson in making religion an every day affair. She was a devout Hindu of the Jain creed, the Puritans of Hinduism (for Hinduism has its denominations even as Christianity). The Jains had four chief doctrines of their faith, all of which are common to Christian beliefs:—

1. Ecstatic devotion to God
2. Fellowship with the universe
3. Service to all
4. Violence to none

One of the first things Gandhi's mother tried to instill into her son was self control, not only in the face of physical danger, but in the face of spiritual and mental danger which she thought much worse. This devout woman trembled to see her son going to the dangerously wicked city of Mother London, where, according to all reports, people ate meat even at the King's table! and where promiscuous social intercourse between men and women, with liquor drinking, was allowed! (Her fears typify unsophisticated motherhood everywhere.) So she would not give her consent for him to go to England to study law until he gave her his threefold vow to eschew wine, women, and meat. This pledge, in spite of his early indulgence and pranks, Gandhi scrupulously kept, thus learning as the first lesson of his new maturity, the control of passion and appetite.

Gandhi in London began to dig deep into Hinduism, Buddhism, and Christianity, and to compare their fundamental philosophies. He attended Christian, Moslem, and Hindu churches. He found there many differences in interpretation, but in their pure essence there was also much similarity between them. He discovered that Buddha and Christ were not mere theorists: they were for direct action in accordance with their creeds. They were not advocates of force as a means of conquest or personal gain; but neither were they cowards, afraid to use strength to fight the force of evil. "What was the greatest thing that Buddha and Christ preached?" asked Gandhi. "Gentleness and love. Yet Buddha fearlessly carried the war into the enemy's camp and brought down on its knees an arrogant priesthood. Christ drove out the money changers from the temple of Jerusalem and drew down curses from Heaven upon the hypocrites and the Pharisees. Both were for intensely direct action, but even when Buddha and Christ chastened wrong-doers they showed unmistakable gentleness and love behind every act of theirs."

Is this so involved, so foreign, so futile, so mystical, that it is impossible for an Englishman or American to understand, as Mr. Chesterton would have us believe? Gandhi has used the religious history of the race merely as a means to bring God down out of the sky into daily life . . . which is also the way of Christian social service. Gandhi's God was not an impersonal being who sat away up on high and waited for the homage of incense and gongs. He was the God of the dusty way; a God of service. Gandhi speaks of God as though he were his friend. Perhaps it is embarrassing to a conventionalized Christian to hear an Indian say, "It was a difficult decision to make but God guided me." But how is this different from our Puritan ancestor who wrote in his diary, "God helped me today over another hard mile"? Here is no complexity but simplicity; the simplicity of the pioneer who knows that nature alone is too much for him, but that God and he together can move mountains.

Gandhi might have adopted Christianity as his church, if it had not been for the attitude of narrow-minded Christians early in his career. There is very strong gossip among his friends that he at one time presented himself at the City

Temple in London for membership, but was discouraged by the officiary because he could not answer all their theological questions to their satisfaction.

One day, during his search for truth in South Africa, Gandhi went with his friend, C. F. Andrews, a former Anglican priest, to the cathedral. The ushers refused to let Gandhi enter because of his color. But the wife of the Bishop happened by.

"Come in, both of you, and sit with me," she said, and swept them in with her to her pew. It was a courageous act on the part of this English woman in the face of the acute color prejudice of South Africa. But the incident did not encourage a sensitive Hindu to believe that all love and truth were contained in the Christian church.

Gandhi himself tells of going to see F. B. Meyer, a noted Christian minister, at the request of his friends. "They thought I was incomplete without acknowledging the message of Christ by joining the Christian church, so they put me in touch with Mr. Meyer. He asked me 'Have you found peace?' 'Yes' I told him. 'Then' said Mr. Meyer, 'I have nothing more to say to you.'"

"The man who casts off all desire and walks without desire . . . comes into peace." This was the peace that Gandhi had found. Overeating, sexual intercourse, material wealth, he had given up as of lesser importance to him than realizing his ideal . . . to teach India that freedom and peace would not come through the killing of other men, but through self-control, personal and national.

Yet Gandhi is frank about the spiritual self-interest that was behind the rôle of reformer which he adopted in South Africa. "If I found myself entirely absorbed in the service of the community the reason behind it was my desire for self-realization" he says. "I had made the religion of service my own, as I felt that God could be realized only through service. And service for me was the service of South Africa, because it came to me without my seeking, because I had an aptitude for it. I had gone to South Africa for travel, for finding an escape from Kathiawar's intrigues and for gaining my own livelihood. But I found myself in search of God and striving for self-realization."

For Gandhi is not an Indian mystic, wrapped in a world beyond a world. He is not an eastern ascetic intent upon making himself one with Nothingness. He is an idealist, who believes in living out his ideals in daily life. He is a practical idealist, with as much accent upon the practical as upon the idealism.

"A clean heart, a clear conscience, regular communion with God, and love for all fellow-men is the way," wrote Gandhi to an American who had written to ask him the remedy for the economic and religious chaos into which our modern world has fallen. "The world is sick unto death with blood spilling. As soon as India accepts the doctrine of the sword my life as an Indian is finished. For it is the weak man who resorts to violence; the strong man who avoids. . . . True, I am a Hindu and not a Christian, but there is more love in my heart for your Christ than there is in the hearts of many who have the audacity to call themselves Christians."

I sat one memorable day of silence in Gandhiji's room. He was reading, meditating, praying, making private lead pencil notes; and occasionally passing some of these slips of rough paper over to me. Not a word was spoken. My New Testament and my Christian communion with God seemed just as normal there as in any church or cathedral. Never has worship been more real.

CHAPTER VII

WHAT'S WRONG WITH FOREIGN MISSIONS?

MISSIONS were born of radical parents. They incarnated a religious Declaration of Independence. They once carried the universal flag of the religious Internationale. Missions of the long ago were fearless, and were so by inheritance. For any one who studies the Bible, realizes that it is a story of fearless prophets.

> "By faith, Moses when he was born was hid three months by his parents because they saw he was a goodly child; *and they were not afraid of the King's commandments.*"

Down through the Hebrew prophets, through Christ and His followers, the thread of fearlessness had been present. Missions had to be unafraid of both church and state because missionaries were so radical in the beginning. The dictionary says that a radical is one who "Holds extreme views or advocates extreme measures." Missions did both, and we who offered ourselves spontaneously, when we were young, to go to the ends of the earth with this banner of the Universal Christ, somehow thought we were radical; thought we had declared our religious independence; thought we were bound to no particular national flag, when its demands conflicted with the flag of this higher allegiance. But the radiant youth of today says that we are moss-backs; that we refuse them the privilege of drafting a declaration of religious independence; that instead of carrying the banner that knows no national flag, we have made out of Christianity a thing subservient to nationalism!

It is a delightful journey to motor to quiet little Williamstown, Massachusetts, the seat of Williams College, and on alighting from our comfortable cars walk up to the monument erected to the men of the Haystack Prayer-meeting. As we look on this monument we feel a stirring pride in the courage of these few men who were the first Americans to decide literally to make the world their parish; a strange sense of vicarious fearlessness comes over us, as though we too had dared all as they did, defying college authorities, friends and family. They had to be radicals to accomplish the impossible, but now, the status quo has become sacrosanct, and we conservatives of middle age will not consent to have it changed in church or state. The hundred years intervening makes it easy to approve of their radical ideas for we have now caught up to them, but somehow it is a little more difficult for us to go with our youth of today.

The list of radicals in early missionary history is a long one. William Carey of England is the most interesting because the most constructive. The young men of Williamstown had made him their hero. If there was ever a man "unafraid of the King's commands," it was William Carey. He tempts one to become an ancestor worshipper; there is a thrill in looking back to this Christian radical. He did such extraordinary things. He became a man without a country. Neither his wife, his church, nor his country could understand why he wanted to go to distant India to preach to the "heathen". His "church" said "If God wanted the 'heathen' converted, He would do it." His "country" said, "If you are going over to India to upset the 'heathen' by changing their religion and their ethics, you cannot ride on our boats; we are there to make money, and we won't have the regime disturbed by education." His "wife" said, "Every day he makes fewer and fewer shoes, but studies more and more in those queer books"; for Carey instead of cobbling all the weary hours spent half his nights at Greek, Hebrew and Sanskrit grammar. Out of scraps of leather he sewed together a map of the world on which he painted the countries and indicated their religions and languages.

His conservative friends shook their heads and said there should be a way of working out this missionary idea that would not call for "such drastic action as to leave everything and go against the better judgment of wise counsel." To church people of England of that day God had already completed his revelation, once and for all time! God was in reality a tribal God, who took part in the gorgeous pageantry of the state Church. Carey was a lonely radical. He was forced to oppose them all.

Strangely, only a short time ago, Gandhi, after one of his many bitter experiences, when foreign Christians and Brahman Hindus stood together against his liberality, said, "A man who starts on the great adventure of truth, must have sufficient faith in himself to do without support from people who do not share his creed."

POST WAR IDEALISTS

Now, again, since the World War, the young missionary has gone out, with the very religion we have taught him, though we never dreamed how well he understood the saints, nor what reality the religion of the fearless had revealed to him. He goes to India. He begins to read his New Testament in the same room with young Indians. He holds the Sermon on the Mount in his hand as he walks with Gandhi through the silent throngs of non-violent Indian villagers. The surging possibility of the Universal Christ comes to him. He goes back to his foreign house where everything speaks of America or Europe. He takes down the foreign trappings and decides to identify his life with Indians. He gives up the eating of meat; like St. Paul, "when meat made his brother to offend". He feels the delicate obligation of a guest in another man's country, and so discards his heavy European clothes and puts on the homespun drapery of the Indian. But the imperialistic government, knowing that the more the sympathetic love of the white man and the brown man merge, the harder it will be for imperialism, issues a mandate that this young missionary leave the country.

So, just as Carey was kept out of India by the then imperialistic government—the East India Company—so now the imperialistic government sends Gordon Halstead and R. R. Keithahn out of India; beats and arrests Dr. Forester Paton of South India.

IMPERIALISM CLAMPS DOWN

Missions were caught napping. In the aftermath of the great World War, when an artificial allegiance was formed among the allies, to the detriment of those we called our "enemies" missions signed away their soul. Every missionary, man or woman, who goes to India from North America, must be vouched for as to his loyalty to the British government, by the Board who pays his salary; otherwise he cannot receive the British visa on his passport. What a travesty upon our modern claim to religious liberty and our scientific insistence upon truth for its own sake.

When the people involved in the Keithahn case asked for an interpretation of the document that the mission Board had signed for their "agents" the British magistrate sent this amazing statement:

"It is the duty not only of every servant of government, no matter in what department he may serve, but also of every person whatever his nationality may be, who belongs to one of these non-official organizations which are permitted by the government to participate in any educational, medical, or other public work in India to show his disapproval of the (nationalist) movement. He is expected to take every opportunity of promoting amongst those with whom he is brought into contact by reason of the activities of the organization to which he belongs loyalty to the government, and countering and exposing by informal talks and discussions the lies, misrepresentations, and economic fallacies that are used in support of the congress program. The government expects this service to be faithfully performed and looks to you as members of such an organization to see that effect is given to this expectation. Any advice that you may require as to the particular methods to be followed will be willingly supplied by me on application." [1]

Is it possible a self-respecting missionary could sell his soul to such a magistracy? Better that every American idealist should withdraw!

FREEDOM SPEAKS

Over against this pagan imperialism stands the Christian manifesto of Verrier Elwin, a discerning British priest—and author of the *Dawn of Indian Freedom.*

1. An Englishman is by definition some one who loves liberty. I am often regarded as disloyal by my fellow-countrymen, but I claim that really it is they who are disloyal, and I am truly loyal to all that is best in the English idea of freedom.
2. I am a follower of Gandhi because I believe he is the greatest living friend of England. I know that his frail unarmed hands are going to destroy her Empire, but I

Christian Century. March 2, 1932.

also know he is going to save her soul. England is committing the terrible sin of oppressing and exploiting India. I long to see her free of that sin. How then can I withhold my allegiance from one who is about to save her from the greatest wickedness that a nation can commit?

3. I support the Congress because I see in its greatest weapon *Satyagraha* the only possible alternative to war in this modern world. Englishmen understand the hatred of an enemy, and they know how to deal with it, but when they meet his love they are bewildered. If you want to court defeat, begin to hate the English. Then you have no chance. But go on loving us, in spite of all, and we can do nothing against you.
4. Finally I am a supporter of the Congress because I believe it is going to usher in a poor man's *Swaraj.* (Government.) I don't know when I was so happy as when I read the declaration of rights adopted by the Karachi Congress. In that *Swaraj* public money will not be wasted on viceregal palaces or on huge armies; it will be given to education, to medical relief, to making life less burdensome to the poor. Then all men will know themselves brothers.[1]

A disciple of Christ, unafraid of the king's commands has just spoken. Men like Elwin, Halstead, Keithahn are free because they are unafraid.

FOREIGN ECONOMIC CONTROL

Self-reliance, as well as freedom, seems to have passed out of the missionary enterprise. The pioneers were self-reliant because the pull of the great idea was more powerful than the

---

[1] *Christian Century.* Aug. 12, 1931.

hindering lack of funds; support took a secondary place. William Carey planted indigo to support his family and to finance the huge task of translation of the Bible into many languages to which he had set himself. William Taylor was another heroic figure who stalked across the horizon of the missionary world along in the seventies. In Australia, in South Africa, in India, and in California, I have met scores of big minded and big souled men and women who became Christian disciples under the rugged winsomeness of this free, self-reliant missionary. He supported his family by dignified manual labor, and much of his work by royalties from books. In America he called for a hundred young men to go to the ends of the earth; without promise of definite support; without guarantee of furlough. He offered them neither easy lives nor easy tasks. Men and women offered themselves from everywhere, some of whom are in India today,—after sixty years. One (of whom I am especially fond) is a grand old figure over eighty years of age. He wears his whiskers William Taylor style, stands as straight as a general, and his aged eyes twinkle with the idealism of youth.

William Carey's and William Taylor's radical ideas have now become a hundred incorporated Boards. In these days we see listed in the appointment offices of state universities a great variety of positions vacant in missionary institutions in all countries of the world. These are discussed nonchalantly by the students as they compare them to a "job" in Detroit, Nashville, or Brockton. They are not moved.

Youth aches for more heroism and a deeper reality than this state-controlled, institutionalized enterprise called missions seems to demand. Once missions were spontaneous and creative. During this epic period the Sermon on the Mount and much of the Bible was translated into over seven hundred languages. The creative work seems to have been done, says the conservative. But that is not enough. That sermon still waits to be translated into life. Toyohiko Kagawa says that Christ must take out His naturalization papers in Japan, and in that one sentence lies creative thought enough for a generation.

When Mahatma Gandhi was asked how Christianity could be naturalized in India, he made a pronouncement to the Christians:

1. All Christians should begin to live more like Christ.
2. Practise your religion without adulterating it or toning it down.
3. Make love control your lives for love is central in Christianity.
4. Study the non-Christian religions more sympathetically to find out what is good in them in order, not to harmonize, but to have a more sympathetic approach to the people.[1]

PROSELYTING

"When India gets self-government" to quote Gandhi still further, "there will be tolerance for all religions . . . but no place for proselyting . . . even by Christian missions." Every word uttered by the Mahatma on the subject of religion, his religion, and especially Christianity, is eagerly devoured by the western world. This last statement set the wires of the world to buzzing. Did this man who calls himself a Hindu, think he had grown so gigantic that he could dictate to the western Christian world? Did this mean that Gandhi was opposed to Christian missions? We must always keep in mind that the educated Indian speaks the English language exceptionally well. He chooses his words with great care for he

[1] Wilson, R. S., *The Indirect Effects of Christian Missions in India.* (London, 1928.)

has learned the language academically, and with his Sanskrit background, has a keen language sense. According to the dictionary there is considerable difference between the word "disciple" and the word "proselyte"; and again between the word "convert" and "disciple". The name "disciple" is given to the follower of a certain faith without reference to previous belief or allegiance; a "convert" is a person who has come to one faith from a different belief or from disbelief; a "proselyte" is one who has been led to accept a religious system whether with or without true faith . . . who is won over to a different religion, sect, or party. Gandhi therefore objects to proselytism but not to discipleship. Conversion to discipleship means changing the direction of a life; as the course of a river is changed to bring fertility, new life to barren fields, but within the same natural environment. Christian proselyting in India, on the contrary, means to pick up a person out of his old landscape and set him down not only with new religious forms, but in alien social conditions. Tolstoy may be said to have been a disciple of Christ when he decided to try to live as Christ lived, although he was a nominal Christian before. A new dynamic had been put into his life . . . but it was a change from within.

Gandhi means exactly what he says when he opposes proselyting. He would not wish to see all the schools or hospitals go. He wants the great surgeon to come as a humanitarian lover of men. He wants him to take out the tumors, to remove the cataracts, to relieve suffering, but to do it as Jesus healed the blind man by the wayside and then said "See that thou tell no man." Jesus did it because he loved humanity. The blind man rose and followed Jesus just because he loved Him. In India it would be the same. The healed man or woman would follow the surgeon to ask the secret of his way of life, and often the patient would accept it, but there would be no paid "agents" who would come and demand that he admit his former error, leave his own community, and join another; no insistence that he be baptized in some form or other; that he cut off the lock of hair on top of his head; nor that he be accounted silly should he refuse to eat meat.

NEW MEN AND NEW FORMS

Why not accept today in the bonds of the Universal Church of Christ such men as Gandhi and Tagore and Natarajan, and myriads of others in India who are literally following the Christ although they have never had a Christian clergyman put water on their heads? The very power that Gandhi wields is living proof of an internal Christian experience. We started new sects down through our history. We have our Presbyterians, Congregationalists, Baptists, Anglicans, Roman Catholics, and Methodists. Why should not the Indians start their own sects where like the Quakers there shall be no baptism or other sacraments required, though all the sacraments could be available for those who desired them. The Indians will greatly enrich our western services eventually by some of the beautiful elements of the Hindu ritual and festival.

Non-Christian rites have enriched Christmas. During the first two centuries of the Christian era the followers did not emphasize the birthday of Christ because all their emphasis was put upon Pentecost and Easter; but later a demand for a celebration of the birthday came and it was at that time that the date was decided upon. It was placed at a time when the great Roman festivals could contribute to it. The Roman Saturnalia was finally blended into Christmas, and the old custom of the slaves being waited on by the masters. The exchanging of gifts at New Year's time, and the great feast of dolls became so dominant in the celebration, that they have continued to this day. The Jewish feast of Lights synchronized with it, and greatly added to the beauty of Christmas. We are just now catching up with that festival. Modern Christmas with its dazzling trees, lighted in the gardens and parks, makes a paradise for both old and young. The Egyptian celebration of the god of Light, with its continuous fire on the altar developed into the hanging of stockings by the fire place. In the Yuletide of the Bretons, Saxons and Norsemen we found Santa Claus.

Picture the enriched Christmas in the orient when without fir trees, and fires, the myriads of *Diwali* lights with their simple little saucers of oil and wicks, shall outline the hut and palace, temple and church, and make the birthday of the Christ eagerly anticipated by every child of India. The Indians are past masters in the art of symbolism, and Christian forms are safe in their religious hands.

At the entrance to one of the great tents which were put up to house the thousands of Nationalist pilgrims who came to attend the 1925 Indian National Congress in Cawnpore, there hung a large framed portrait of Christ on the Cross; and every Hindu, every Moslem, every Jain, and every Sikh who passed through that entrance gazed at the picture with reverence. Many of them stopped and bowed their heads. Over several doorways of shops surrounding the Congress tent were signs "Believe in God". The Hindu not only takes *his* religion seriously; he takes *your* religion seriously.

IMPERIALISM

Missions are suffering from imperialism; and "efficiency" is the little god that has caused much of the trouble. The Indians, it is claimed, are simply not efficient; they cannot keep up the property; they do not know how to run an organization; and so long as we send money from this side of the world, just so long shall we dictate what shall be done with it, even though we do it at a distance of six, or eight, or ten thousand miles away.

If the Indians are not able to keep up the foreign buildings after we have taught them for a hundred years, then there is something wrong with the buildings, and not with the Indians. If Indian women are not capable of becoming the principals of schools for girls, then there is something wrong with the type of institution we have built; for they have been studying in colleges now for fifty years. "There will never be a time when India will not require foreign missionaries" is a refrain we hear on every hand. It may be that there will be for many years to come white followers of Christ who will wish to cast in their lot with India, but they will necessarily be men of India's choosing—not sent out regardless of their fitness to identify their lives with the people they serve.

Lord Curzon, when Viceroy of India, planning for the great Coronation Durbar at Delhi, forbade the singing of "Onward Christian Soldiers" because he feared two lines of it might reflect upon imperial power!

> "Crowns and thrones may perish
> Kingdoms rise and wane:"

That immense royal show was to demonstrate the imperishability of the empire, and not one word of doubt must be spoken or even sung in a Christian hymn. So it seems youth is disloyal if it speaks of the time when the throne of the white missionary may perish, or the kingdom of foreigners wane. But, irony of fate! that hymn is now being expunged from our hymnals for military turpitude.

CHANGE THE EMPHASIS

India with its emphasis on non-violence finds it very difficult to swallow the unthinking use of military terms in the missionary movement. Literature goes out from the G.H.Q. in London and New York that speaks of "front line trenches"; "the home base"; "the far-flung battle line"; and "recruiting agencies". Young missionaries go out "under marching orders". New churches in the far away countries have been looked upon as "colonies" of the supporting churches at home. Somehow missions have fallen victims to the spirit of conquest, when they should have been content with an expanding growth. The expansion has been superimposed from without when it should have come from a change within.

Probably the deepest thing that is wrong with foreign missions is that it is FOREIGN. Foreign dictation; foreign organization; foreign churches; foreign music; foreign hymns; foreign education; foreign clothes; foreign everything.

The modern missionary is not sent out to induce the Hindu to exchange his own social system for a western mode of living, but to show him Christ's way of life. And yet the Indian Christian is already so compromised that he can be scarcely more than a carbon copy of his western Christian teacher. That is, in effect, why the Indian Christian women have lost their leadership in all social reforms of the country; they are so Anglicized that they may be said to have little Indian background left. The missionary who consistently identifies his life with Indian aspirations, and who adapts his habits to his Indian environment will be the most successful. There is no inconsistency between living the Indian life and the Christ life.

But at the present time when one tries to wear Indian clothes, to teach Indian cultural backgrounds, and to sympathize with present day Indian attitudes, he not only comes under suspicion but is likely to be deported as an undesirable alien. In some mysterious fashion he has injured the sensitive "white prestige" in a way that the drunken white man, kicking his Indian coolie about, has been unable to accomplish. At least the drunken upholder of the white man's superiority is not deported.

Clothes may seem a superficial thing, and yet they have in some instances become a test of culture. Mr. H. E. Hwang, the present Chinese Ambassador to Vienna, a man of great dignity in China, tried to be a Chinese gentleman when he was in this country some years ago. But the boys on Wall Street so hooted at his magnificent Chinese robes, that he was forced to adopt American dress. In China and India, the politeness of the people allows all of us Europeans to wear what we like as well as to trample on their sensibilities without our even being conscious of it.

To the man who is familiar with the slow measured cadences of Indian life, there is nothing quite so ironical as the rattling Ford grinding through the streets of a quiet little Indian town, throwing out pamphlets entitled, "Peace on earth". "Just think how efficient a car would make a worker" is the cry of the mission agency. He can cover ten towns instead of one in a day; so he goes honking his horn from meeting to meeting. Between his visits the town sees nothing faster than a bullock cart at two miles an hour. And when the Ford passes, all the gossip of the village centers around these wildly uncivilized foreigners, belching fire and throwing out little papers on peace.

No, this is not the most effective way in vast, quiet, deeply thinking India, to teach of the gentle Nazarene. It will need to be done in a way that more nearly approaches the Indian spirit.

In case of international disputes it would be infinitely better business to have title to all properties in the hands of citizens. If vandals destroyed a mission compound as is possible in Nanking or Calcutta, it would then be a question for the local government to adjust with the local people, rather than an international question to be taken up and settled by unwelcome indemnities in far away capitals. But apart from any complications in the realm of politics or ownership, the churches, schools, and hospitals belong to the people for whom and to whom they were given by generous disinterested Christians.

Administration from a distant base, eight, ten, or twelve thousand miles away, holding control because of investments, will never build up the Christian church in the orient.

TRUTH GOES MARCHING ON

Perhaps these paragraphs are more of a confession than a criticism. I have been a part of this system for a quarter of a century. To advance such ideas is not to deprecate the amazing influence for good of missions yesterday and today. The new social order that has come to India owes its inception chiefly to the intrepid servants of Christ, who trekked across the world in pilgrimages of peace and good-will both passionate and scientific. K. Natarajan, editor of the "Indian Social Reformer", Bombay, says that social service achievements in India may be said to have resulted from the advent into India of modern protestant Christian missionaries.

"Don't worry about Christian missions" said a thoughtful Indian to me recently; "When the British government is gone and the imperial policy of the white man is discouraged, thousands of Indians will come out openly as followers of Christ. The lid of the volcano will be lifted and real Christianity, neither brown nor white, will naturally assert itself."

Have we failed, then, in our missionary program? Far from it. There is nothing wrong with the ideal of missions, but the results accomplished have leaped so far ahead of our administrative organization that we have to run to keep up with them.

Today may be the greatest hour that missions have ever experienced; the masses have become articulate; the social order is changing. Christ has become so real, so vital, that a new expression of his living life is here. Old methods and old forms are no longer necessary. Missions have served their apprenticeship. Now the full day of indigenous Christian life is dawning. It is not a question of pressing a cause onward to victory, but of having the grace to step aside and let the truth sweep forward.

CHAPTER VIII

SEX IN INDIA

"I'M GOING to live! I'm going to live!"

Tearing through the thin veils of pre-history comes this cry from the primitive heart of India. This passionate psalm rose from the first humans who sat down upon the vast, hot, steaming plain; it swelled above their heroic struggle with climate, disease, and death. It culminated in a veritable diapason of terrible desire. "Life!" "Life!" This was India's first necessity; it was also her first religious chant.

That the garden of Eden was in India there is no scientific means to prove. One great authority assigned Adam and Eve to the North Pole! But it seems to be the consensus of opinion that the biological cradle of the race was at least not far from India. Certain it is that long before the spotlight of history was focused upon this part of the east, the human race had been for centuries fighting the ruthless force of the tropics for mere existence.

The germs of life in this seething tropical plain were insistent; but the seeds of death were almost equally strong. Climate has been the black god of India. It has vitally influenced the development of the entire race—religiously, nationally, and racially. The most adverse conditions in the world for nurturing human life have meant that man's struggle for survival was intense and agonizing. Disease, fostered by heat, rain, drouth, and famine, following each other in rapid succession, stretched jealous fingers for each new life. There was in those days no medicine, no hygiene, no knowledge of good and evil—simply an instinctive determination to prolong and multiply life. *"I will live"*, gasped this struggling man. Thus grew up the first use of human will power, an emergence from the biological urge. What was the answer to this determination? Obviously, as many babies as possible. Twenty babies must be born that one might mature.

Promiscuous mating was then the natural rule of life. The father did not even know that he was the father of children, but the mother carried the proof of relationship in her own body. So a system of matriarchy developed. The mothers of the race became the rulers, the holders of property, the sacred possession of the tribe.

After a time when the relation of the sex act to the coming of children became evident, the responsibility of the father developed, and social and family consciousness was born among the tribes of India. Still the urge to multiply and conquer their environment grew stronger and stronger. Here was a vast continent to be tamed to the hand of man, that must be made to grow his food, sustain his life. Any process that would aid life was sanctioned; wrong was death, right was life. A man could not have enough sons to labor in the fields if he had only one woman; so he took to himself several wives. Girl children must begin to produce as soon as possible that the march of man's conquest over the earth might go on. Thus child marriage and polygamy grew up as normal developments.

Polygamy, however, is not the unique inheritance of India. These practises have grown up wherever there have appeared similar biological and economic necessities. The early Jews, for example, were polygamous. They needed sons to till their fields, to tend their vast herds. Therefore, from Abraham straight down there is no terrible condemnation of polygamy in the Old Testament. Sarah was even praised for giving Hagar to Abraham so that he might have a son.

Mormonism in America grew out of the same sort of causes as polygamy in India, only in a later age. People, many laborers, strong sons and daughters were needed to populate the western prairies. But since these new conquerors of a continent needed psychological courage to meet public opinion, they gave their polygamous experiment the sanction of God. During the covered wagon period these pioneers crowded from New York to Kansas, and then pressed on to Utah. Their many children, white, virile, not only conquered the land, but soon came to be political, religious, educational powers throughout the new west. They invaded the Senate.

There are reformers in this country who think that it was their outcry which stifled polygamy in America. But to look at Mormonism in the cold light of environmental history is to see simply the fact of a rising tide of European immigration that spread from east westward and from the west eastward, bringing with it an abundance of population and labor. Thus the biological pull of an unsettled continent was satisfied and polygamy died. It is always difficult to see ourselves as others see us.

Out of climatic, economic and biological necessity grew the social and religious sanctions of sex practises in India. When primitive men began to realize that some unknown power within or beyond the sex act made one woman fertile, and disgraced another by barrenness; that made one man a father, and denied another children, they began to revere the power of fertility. Phallic worship began.

The fight against climate and environmental death led normally to the belief that God worked through the organs of life. Germs of death abounded. Babies died. Humidity, plague, cholera, smallpox—before these diseases were ever even given names—became incarnated demons. Evil was most clearly conceived of as disease and death, whilst good and God were united in the forces of life. These were days of animism when the fateful facts of life were fateful spirits at work. Sun and rain, storm and calm, day and night, body and soul, were all pictured as spirit activity and incarnation. These we forget. But morbid interest makes us hot on the trail of phallic symbols.

SEX WORSHIP

Idolatry in India was just an attempt to make real the conception of god power. This led to sex-worship in the temples. The male organ made possible the conception of children. It was therefore the symbol of creative god power; idols were made of the lingam. Cults or sects grew up about this worship of a natural function. The male came also to worship the female sex organ to ask that the spirit of birth and fertility for which this stood might bring to him and his family the gifts of life. Groveling or uncultured as this sort of worship may seem from our present outlook on life, it was a natural corollary of the racial struggle of this people under adverse conditions.

Our cultural inheritance from Greece has eased our reading of Greek history and mythology at this point. The early Greeks had great religious processions, like our modern parades with floats, wherein the phallus, the image of the male organ, was carried by priests and maidens. The Roman lingam has similar primitive associations. Ten centuries of Roman Christianity did not stamp it all out. What missionary among educated non-Christian groups has ever failed to be reminded of the rule of harlots in the papal court of the tenth century, when Theodora and her daughter Marozia established a veritable pornocracy over a Christian world through sexual profligacy? We accept this historical fact for just what it is, but no more. Indian instances must likewise be seen in their true perspective.

The temple in this early India was at once the place of worship, the town hall, the market place, the forum of religion, politics, and education. The temple walls were the school books of this new race, and since it was the highest morality to have as many children as possible, the walls were used to explain the most approved methods of obtaining healthy progeny. In the same dramatic way Christianity was later to use the miracle plays of the middle ages to depict to an unlettered common people the concepts of that religion.

SEX INSTRUCTION

Many of these temple pictures and inscriptions now shock modern eyes. It is a curious fact however, that the scientific and psychological books of modern Europe and America telling (with diagrams) how to have satisfactory marital relationships often go back to and sanction these very methods which the Indian temples tell. Indians and Arabians developed early in history a clear understanding of the sex act and of its relationship to the family and society. We are reminded of this by a recent scientific treatise upon the technique of marriage which has for its introduction a quotation from no less a personage than the Archbishop of Canterbury.

Is it logical, sensible, or even ethical for the western world to get so excited over the fact that Indians have dealt practically with this phase of life when we ourselves are just beginning to realize that we must face sex openly? We talk about "the technique of married life" and are "scientific and psychological." The Indian uses ordinary words and we vote him horrible.

We are dealing with a problem as old as the ages. The purpose of our scientific approach to sex today is to make it possible for people to have healthy children and to teach that it is our right and privilege to have sexual pleasure within the bonds of matrimony without the responsibility of children. Books like these are in all our college centres, as well as in our private and public libraries. The only difference between us and the east is that India developed a crudely scientific technique at the time when she most needed it, and we are developing ours in terms of modern demands.

This is not a plea for our adoption of the Indian methods and sexual ideals. The modern educated Indian is himself abandoning these as unfitted to the new day. India today no longer needs population but birth control. She no longer has any economic necessity for child marriage and polygamy. Hence these practises are on the wane.

I shall never forget how a young Hindu priest drew himself up when asked about some ancient sexual paintings which used to be visible upon the walls of his monastery, old pictures with soft rich colors tempered by the centuries, priceless from an artistic viewpoint. "Nobody today asks to see those pictures except foreigners" he said. "We young priests think it unfair for our temple to just give a sex thrill to tourists. So we have whitewashed the paintings out." Moreover, India, not having a prudish Puritan attitude towards sex, but regarding it as a normal act of life, will with rapid and intelligent social constructiveness adopt birth control, monogamy, and mature marriage. Three hundred and fifty millions of people cannot be expected to change their way of living in a day, but the trend is unmistakably towards scientific control.

This is true because the very same causes that made polygamy unnecessary in America are operating in modern India. Christian missionaries, the British government, and modern scientific education have played their important part in bringing about the dawning of the new day in India. But the underlying cause for change is economic. With the coming of sanitation, education, preventive medicine, the average length of life of the Indian has increased. Therefore not so many new births are required. The result is that polygamy is declining, although the population is actually increasing due to a lengthening span of life. The next generation will see a real decrease in the number of children born. This is already under way with the agitation against child marriage, and the recent Sarda Marriage Act, raising the legal age of marriage for a girl to 14, and for a boy to 18. The government hesitated too long over these bills which were before them for years. Powerful Mohammedans, whose good-will the British law-makers wished to keep, were against them, and year after year went by when the Bill was set aside. But enlightened Hindu opinion finally won the day and in April 1930 the famous Sarda Marriage Act became a reality. Enlightened Indian opinion will gradually enforce these laws and make them potent.

Indian opinion is also tearing away the *purdah,* the veil, from womanhood. I have attended great religious and social conferences in India within the last five years at which from four hundred to two thousand Indian women were present . . . and there was not one veil. Many of these women, college graduates, would come forward as naturally as the men to debate an issue. Banners floated over the women's delegation, bearing the slogans,

"EDUCATION FOR WOMEN"

"COMPULSORY EDUCATION FOR ALL CHILDREN"

"DISCARD YOUR VEIL"

"VOTES FOR WOMEN"

At dinners held in the evening after these daily sessions, these women acted as hostesses to educated men of all castes and creeds. Not a veil was worn. These were patriotic modern banquets, such as might be held in any ball room in Detroit, New York, or San Francisco. Every division was lost in the great ideal of being an Indian; the consciousness of nationality had broken down social and religious barriers.

THE ZENANA

This taking of the veil, or separation of the Indian women from the men was partly a gift of Mohammedanism to India, and partly the result of the great life urge which held women, as the mother of the race, precious and sacred. It was originally a beautiful concept. In the early days, instead of a straw roof, a stone roof was put over the woman's quarters to protect her from the heat. Man moved about from place to place, but woman was static, except for small daily errands. She had to have cool and shade. Also as she went about in the bazaars she must be protected from disease; for all sorts of malignant terrors stalked the streets, and reached out from the alleys. To protect her from the lepers who thronged the market places, from the contaminating touch, the woman drew her veil about her. The full veil, or *burka,* covers the whole dress like a robe. The urge of passion in this hot tropical country where nature has been so prodigal in her gestures that she sows a hundred shoots to raise one high bamboo, seemed to make it necessary for women to be protected from the eyes of men other than their kinsmen. Perhaps only those who have lived in the tropics, who have experienced the warm vital rays of a luxuriant sun, with living colors that cry aloud, and exotic perfume from the breast of nature, can understand how necessary this *purdah* was in those early days of passion, stimulated not only by nature, but by social needs.

But as life changed in its dangerous aspects, and modern society developed, women by the veil were consciously denied many of the greatest interests in life; and *purdah* became a curse for India. It is an anachronism under modern conditions, and is eventually doomed. But women are the conservatives of every race, and it is only through example and patient education that *purdah* will be entirely abolished. I have seen women graduates of Christian colleges go up to get their diplomas in the long veil, so great is the force of custom.

But, on the other hand, women of the highest rank are tearing away the veil, to work for Indian freedom. Most college girls in India know the veil as little as do our American college students. In Calcutta the women's colleges are associated with the university and the women are allowed to attend classes with the men. They get their degrees on the English Cambridge standard, from the same text books, in the same language, and from the same point of view as the men. They know perhaps as much about the world in general as do our intelligent American or English girls. The only difference between the woman college graduate in Calcutta and Boston is the size of the job the Indian girl has before her.

The scientific era goes back only a couple of centuries. Our western women are children of this scientific era, and of the comparatively recent European renaissance. So they have inherited only a few hundred years of a comparatively simple social growth. But the Indian college girl has inherited over six thousand years of complex social forms, developed as a defense against climatic hardship. The background of her life has been slowly evolving, undisturbed by outside conditions, for thousands of years. It is therefore manifestly unfair to blame upon the present generation of educated modern Indian women all they have inherited out of an adverse and complex past.

Before launching upon a wholesale denunciation of India, therefore, because of her religious and sex traditions, it behooves the western world to consider all the facts. There are as many people in India today living under monogamy as the whole population of the United States. Gandhi, the outstanding statesman of the new east, has never had but one wife. Tagore, the leading intellectual of India, has had but one wife. There are millions of Indians who take the classic vow to "cleave only unto her so long as both shall live." Only they cleave a little longer than we do because of their ideal of the sanctity of the family. Under Hindu law, as under the Roman Catholic, divorce is difficult. There is more divorce in the State of Nevada than among the hundreds of millions of India.

CHILD MARRIAGE

Gandhi himself was betrothed at the age of eight years, and married when he was but thirteen years of age. He himself says that he wasted that first year of marriage, so far as his schooling was concerned, trying to adjust himself to the new conditions of life. He has never ceased regretting the time which carnal indulgence took from what he considers more important things of the spirit. He has gone the whole gamut of experience from unrestrained license (if you can call it that when a husband remains faithful to one wife for half a century) of the boy husband to the strict continence which he now practises.

He took the vow of continence, chastity, during his struggle to win human rights for his Indian compatriots in South Africa. He has held strictly to it for fifteen years.

This same vow is required of his intimate followers who live at his Ashram at Ahmedabad. Gandhi believes that while sexual intercourse between husband and wife is natural and right, nevertheless when a man or woman has vowed himself or herself to the pursuit of a great national and spiritual ideal, he cannot afford to cumber himself with family ties. "If my wife had been going to have a baby when I was about to be sent to prison for holding to my beliefs, how could I stick to the truth and see her starve?" he asked himself in those early days back in South Africa. So he and his wife talked the matter over and agreed to be abstinent co-workers together for truth and freedom. She became his political lieutenant and mothered his ideals with the same sweetness of spirit with which she had mothered his children.

Speaking from experience then, Gandhi, with thousands of educated Indians, does not believe in child marriage for India. "Children born of such early unions are apt to be physically weak" he remarks. "Too early marriage leads to extravagant sexual indulgence, which is a bad thing whether in or out of marriage bonds. There is a certain character, a strength which comes only from self-control." It is because the white race has had the ideal of continence before marriage that it has remained physically stronger.

"But" asks Gandhi slyly, "do you westerners think you have solved the sex problem? It is true that in child marriage we have legitimatized self-indulgence. Yet child marriage was originally designed to protect the girl child of the race. You frown socially upon sexual intercourse before marriage . . . and rightly. But nearly every white man to whom I have talked seriously about the matter has confessed to some form of sexual indulgence before marriage. Your ideals are right, but your practise is faulty."

Then with gentle courtesy to his wife he adds, "My sort of marriage cannot be rotten to the core when my wife and I have found such beauty in our years together. Is not our congeniality at least partly due to our early marriage which permitted our two personalities to merge in a way which would have been impossible for two mature people who marry with their individual bents already set? My wife still moves me as no other woman in the world can. Not that she has no faults . . . or that I have none. But the feeling of an indissoluble bond is there." And this is the Indian Hindu talking! Could a British Christian pay his wife a higher tribute? Is our American attitude towards marriage, when we have one divorce for every six weddings, so much superior?

Nor is it fair for us of the west to condemn the Indian because he gave religious sanction to his biological necessities. Many Indians refuse our Bible as a holy book because of the Old Testament. They think that because Jehovah was a god of battles, and because some of the practises of the old Hebrew fathers were nefarious from the modern point of view, that the Bible is unmoral. We ourselves know that it is out of the tribal god of the Jews that later Christian ideals developed. The Old Testament Bible is not just a book but a library of brief books produced in successive ages, bound into one volume. The Hindu sacred books, which we condemn because of misunderstood oriental conceptions, are also libraries, portraying the religious development of the race. But if we therefore condemn the Mahabharata, the sacred epic of Hinduism, as unmoral, can we blame the Hindu for his critical view of our Bible, deducing therefrom the idea that Christianity sanctions polygamy, war, slavery, drunkenness? We have no Bible with foot-notes saying, "Do not believe this" or "Skip over that".

POLYGAMY

Moslem protagonists always remind us that certain American Christians have approved polygamy. Mormonism is an indigenous religious cult developed in America. The Mormons call themselves the "latter day saints" . . . thus claiming, in Moslem eyes, a revelation higher than other Christian denominations. They gave the name "Independence" to their first home in Kansas because they felt they had a finer, higher, more independent religious interpretation of the Scriptures than any other group.

"Oh but that is not real Christianity" says some shocked reader. "Polygamy is not based upon the teachings of Christ. Christian civilization as a social system may have permitted polygamy in Mormonism for a while, but not as an essentially Christian religion!" Just so. But Hinduism is also a social system. If it had not been so, all the racial customs and needs, what we today call abuses, in the way of sex worship, would not have grown up about the temple. Polygamy, child marriage, the veil, phallic symbols are not essential to the pure religious philosophy of Hinduism. These are biological growths, sanctioned, but extraneous, detachable, which wither when they have served their social and economic purposes. Scientific renaissance changes things.

I have deliberately included in this study of modern India and her prophet-statesman a frank interpretation of the background of sex because so much of our recent popularized literature on Indian life and civilization has morbidly exaggerated sex relationships and practises. The country is too old, and the successive layers of civilization overlap too much for shallow, travelling observers to separate the dead and dying vestiges from the living society. There are in all growing, changing civilizations such things as vestigial social customs. It is a literary crime to brilliantly and seductively describe these dying elements in such manner as to betray the true national character. Will Durant has shown a lot of sense by laughing at these lurid sex descriptions. He says that the pornographic propagandists against India had so stirred his male imagination on this subject that he experienced a humorous disappointment not to find sex more openly apparent as he travelled through India! One would think it hung on trees, was displayed in store windows, and draped the very horizon.

The naked girls on our American bill-boards and magazine covers, the stories and novels of modern Europe, and the motion picture dramas would shock and frighten the modest debutantes of cultured Hindu homes.

IDEALISM IN SEX

It is a curious fact that the biological reverence for life which had given India its sex emphasis, was also to be the root of its highest idealism. "I'm going to live!" cried the primeval Indian. The next step was, "I want others to live. I will not kill." So great was his respect for life that the Indian would not slaughter animals for food, and certainly he would not destroy human beings. Out of this early respect and passion for life has come the creative idealism of modern India. We call the doctrine non-violence. Its name is *Ahimsa*.

Ahimsa means not only life for oneself, but for others. Translated as one word it would read "harmlessness". To get its full significance however, one must use an entire English sentence— "I will not cripple or kill any living creature to benefit my own life." This implies the kind of humanitarian love exemplified by both Buddha and Jesus. It is also intrinsically modern in its appeal, for the universal cry of modern goodwill is to live and let live. It is the only practical plan of international living, for without this ideal, tolerance and cooperation are dead symbols.

Ahimsa lay deep down in the soul of the Indian people. Mothers and fathers had taught this doctrine to their children, generation after generation. Whether they had succeeded entirely in living up to this ideal in their daily life is questionable; but at least this was the catechism held up before the Hindu baby from the time it could lisp. Life had cost the Hindu too high a price to under-value it, even in an enemy.

The primitive struggle for life that brought India the blight of sex indulgence, which tended to emasculate her youth, and to make them subject to the strong sword of the white race, had developed also the highest degree of idealism. Born of the flesh, the worship of life itself rose to the high selflessness of *Ahimsa*.

It remained for Mohandas Gandhi to seize upon this living idealism of a tenacious people and to beat its moral force into a sword. When Gandhi wanted to lay hold of Indian public opinion he took this ideal of *Ahimsa*, rooted through the centuries, as his anchor. It is because he is the living example of this kindly Hindu ideal that he is able today to control more millions than any living king or ruler. He is India's human god.

CHAPTER IX

MADAME GANDHI

THE women of India are waging war. The Sunday rotogravure picture of the woman warrior is usually that of a large boned Russian peasant in overalls, whose hair has been bobbed with a jack knife. But this woman warrior of India is a combination of the gentility of Joanne of Arc, and the cultured grace of Mumtaz Mahal, in whose memory Shah Jahan built the Taj Mahal, the most beautiful building in the world.

The Indian women have donned no uniform—unless *khaddar,* the Indian homespun, may be so named. They will all be found wearing homespun cloth, woven by their own hands, draped in the same soft, graceful, even flattering *sari* that all women of all creeds in India have worn for ages. These women are not "enjoying the war", they are waging it. Their specialties are not the ordinary womanly war duties: they are not doing nursing, or stenography, or operating telephone switchboards, or entertaining the troops. They are fighting, as the men are fighting, in a war of passive resistance. They have a stark realization of the dangers they run. Madame Mohandas Gandhi herself has gone to prison, and thousands of her most cultivated compatriots were there with her. For even a bloodless war is grim business.

The western world has so many trappings when it goes to war. It has to have tanks, field pieces, airplanes, hangars, camps, dugouts, uniforms, camp cooks, and all the endless military supplies which we saw landed in France. The Indian women have entered, however, into a silent war of ideas: their chief weapon a silent insistence upon truth. An insistence to the death. Although these women may use invisible weapons their argument is reasonable—

"With thousands of our Indian men and women pouring out of the numerous universities where they have taken Cambridge-equivalent degrees, we can now decide how much we shall be taxed; how these taxes shall be spent. We insist that our cotton which we grow in such large quantities and of such high quality, shall no longer need to take the little jaunt over-seas to Lancashire, be made up in cloth there, and be returned to us in expensive bolts. We can spin it here at home."

So the women's coat-of-arms is a spinning wheel. Spinning has spread over India as rampantly today as contract-bridge over America. India has the men who can build the factories; she has the steel that can make the necessary spindles; she has the men and women who can operate and manage the factories. Heretofore, as soon as the cotton left her hands she had nothing to do until the expensive bolts came back from Lancashire, and therefore the Indian people were turned into the largest army of unemployed in the world. Even when the costly English-woven bolts of cloth came back, the Indians had no money to buy them. Therefore, spin. The women have taken it up. With one whirr of the wheel, they pray—*Satyagraha*—silent insistence upon truth—with the next, they sing "Hail to the Mother-land!"

> "My Motherland I sing; thou art the head,
> Thou art my heart. . . .
> Before thy feet I bow!"

India, to many militant visitors, radiates a feminine atmosphere. "They take the thing lying down" the man of the west says— "They haven't the guts to fight." But under the surface there is steel as hard as that of any gatling gun. Any fighting pacifist is a new creature in the world. A woman fighting pacifist still newer. Woman in India today walks softly out of her inner apartments to do picketing in front of the liquor and opium shops. And always she spins, whether behind the purdah, or out in the thick of the open struggle; and when she spins she turns a wheel heard round the world.

If India and Indian men are lacking in masculine western pugnacity (and it may be so) they have that amazing womanly quality which Benjamin Kidd describes in his dynamic book "The Science of Power". He says that our whole psychology down through the centuries has been for A to kill B before B could kill A. Every test of manhood and power was made on that basis. But an outstanding feminine quality, because of the nature of woman's relationship to the next generation, was able to sacrifice the present to the future; to sacrifice individualism to the good of the family and the race.

A GIRL WIFE

Sacrifice and devotion have been the key notes of the character of Kastarbai Gandhi. She was betrothed to Mohandas Gandhi when she was only eight years old, and she came to live with the Gandhi family when she was but eleven, which means that she had very much the same childhood training and upbringing as her husband.

Gandhi's mother was the second wife of her husband, who was treasurer first of the small native state of Porbandar, and then of Rajkot. The first wife had died. The second Mrs. Gandhi was a woman of great power socially in Porbandar, and being a very close friend of the court ladies, she became no mean power in politics. She was not fond of jewelry, and as one of Gandhi's biographers says, "She wore comparatively little adornment, just the usual nose rings, with bangles of ivory on her wrists and heavy anklets." Certainly sufficient for an American woman, but not so stupendous when one considers that an Indian wife usually wears a large part of her husband's fortune on her person. She was very religious, and carried her zeal to great lengths through her powerful personality. There was whispered a rumor in the town that she had fasted for seven days at a time; yet in spite of her stern discipline, the children, including Kastarbai, clung to her with boundless affection.

Madame Gandhi mothered the town. Since she was a member of the Brahman caste, if a Brahman were ill or in trouble, she would go to her. But miracle though it seems now, if an outcaste were ill, she would also go and nurse her all night, or night after night if necessary. India has always had her beggars, and prosperous Porbandar had not a few of them who all knew that always at the gateway of the Gandhi estate, flanked on either side by the temples of Krishna and Rama, they would receive either some alms, or a cup of whey. No beggar was ever turned away from its door.

One of the rooms in this huge rambling house was given over to worship; a light was always burning there; and offerings of flowers lay on the altar. And Madame Gandhi's first duty in the morning, after bathing, was to go to the sacred room for recital of her *mantras*. Religion was the first law of family life.

True to their religion, the Gandhis consulted the family astrologer who looked up the signs of the zodiac and made a reckoning by the stars, and found that the two children, Kastarbai and Mohandas, would be happy together! And so in 1877 the betrothal was celebrated. A betrothal with these old families of India is as sacred and as binding as is the wedding ceremony.

The joint family system in operation in India means that all the sons bring their brides to their father's home, though few of them bring their fiancées as Gandhi did. The bride's parents do not have to go to the expense of a wedding. Why should they when they are giving the groom's people the present of a new daughter! The groom's family pays all the wedding expenses, although the bride brings some dowry in the way of jewelry, embroidered quilts, and a trousseau of beautiful saris and lingerie, to her husband's home. She has also been the recipient on the betrothal day of anklets, nose rings, ear rings of gold, and bracelets of ivory and gold, the number being limited only by the purse of the family.

Although Kastarbai and Mohandas had played together for two years, things on the wedding day were as ceremonious as though they had never seen each other. It took place in the old family home at Porbandar, at the same time as the wedding of his cousin and of one of Mohandas's older brothers. The Gandhis had owned this house for generations, and as some of the former families had been large the ancestors had been obliged to add many more apartments than the original house warranted. After they made as many additions to the first floor as possible, then they carried the house up until the fourth story was reached. Like the others in the town, it was built of white stone quarried in the neighborhood. Hardened by exposure so that it had the appearance of a solid block of marble, it had endured for hundreds of years. Snowy houses of this kind, glittering under an Indian sun, had given Porbandar the name of "the white city."

The sea was in sight of the Gandhi house, and had been the family's nursing mother. Here the Gandhi boys sniffed the salt air and watched the Indian seagoing vessels made, ships that were to beat against the winds of Zanzibar and Aden, to sail to Africa and Arabia.

What wonder therefore if the greatest of the Gandhi clan was later to cross the "black water" to London and to Africa?

It was into this adventurous Gandhi clan that the little girl Kastarbai was married. Into the city of Porbandar the wedding procession came. The Gandhis had had to come over from Rajkot where they had been living for some time, because the wedding could not rightly take place at any place other than the old ancestral estate. In fact the father of Mohandas was unable to get leave of absence until so near the wedding day that in the haste of travel by relays of horses between the two cities, his cumbersome chariot overturned and he sustained injuries from which he never recovered.

The little bride wearing a veil for the first time in her life was brought into town in a palanquin. Wedding feasts lasted for days, and presents were brought by a multitude of relatives who had been coming into the old city of Porbandar for days—some on camels, some in palanquins, and some in horse-drawn chariots. In fact some of them came weeks before the marriage ceremony. Flowers were everywhere. Priests from both temples, Krishna and Rama (these temples almost adjoined the house) were there chanting their *mantras*. The bride's palanquin was set down in the open court, and the women relatives came out to greet her. They walked through the open court, up a raised veranda, and finally into the large rambling Gandhi house, which was to be the future home of the bride. Conch shells were blown from the upper verandas to welcome her. Flower petals were thrown over her head and over the palanquin from which she had alighted. They were tossed to her also by numerous child relatives who had come too to take part in the gay and festive occasion. Her pathway was literally covered with flower petals from the outer court until she reached the ceremonial room. The scent of jasmine and lilies was heavy. Color was everywhere—the color of the women's saris, the gayety of the boys' skirts and gorgeously embroidered caps. Garlands of flowers were put over her head, and the air was humming with the chanting of human voices and the strumming of musical instruments.

After Kastarbai and her boy bridegroom had taken the seven steps together, her veil was lifted. According to the usual custom he would have looked upon her face then for the first time. He probably feigned great surprise as her face appeared, but since they had had many a game of cowrie shells together, and probably many a scrap, they were, in reality well-acquainted comrades already.

The most beautiful apartment in the great old house was set aside for the bride and groom. Mohandas, the shy little fellow wore a gayly embroidered cap, coat and sandals, and Kastarbai a beautiful silk sari, fine muslin lingerie, and her heavy jewelry. Thus they started out in life together.

This year the Gandhis will celebrate their fiftieth wedding anniversary in the Poona jail! They are both incarcerated there as passive resisters. The black hair of that long ago little girl has turned gray, and her mouth is sunken but firm. Yet Kastarbai Gandhi still retains traces of a rare beauty. Her large head is set nobly on her shoulders; she holds herself proudly erect, and still though over sixty, has a physique of great strength. It has been fifteen years since she led that famous march of those first women passive resisters from the Ashram at Phoenix, Africa, to the jail in the Transvaal. Yet she is still strong, unconquered. Polygamy and purdah have never been practised in the strong line of the Gandhis, so Kastarbai has had to be many wives to her small world-shaking husband. And as one looks at her wide low forehead, cut with deep lines of suffering, and at her large burning sunken black eyes, one perceives that the years have granted Kastarbai Gandhi for her pain, two compensations—tenderness and sympathy. Hers is the face over again that stares out of medieval paintings, the translucent patient face of the mother of God.

Gandhi at first did not dream the power of will and the scope of character that was wrapped up in the modest, shy slip of a girl he had married. He has often confessed that as a lad of thirteen, instead of a protecting bride-groom, he was a scared youth afraid of the dark; afraid of ghosts; and of serpents. And he found it nettled him as a male to have a wife, his own age, sleeping at his side, who could go anywhere in the dark, and know no fear—even of serpents or of ghosts. That young fearless wife was not only to bear his sons, but to be his comrade in battle in many a weary march. She too is scarred with the struggle for "truth", both in South Africa and again in India.

MOTHERHOOD

Mrs. Gandhi has done her duty also as an Indian mother. She has four sons—Harilal, Ramdas, Monilal and Devadas. The three latter have been working side by side with their father and mother for the freedom of India ever since they were old enough to reach their own decisions. But the oldest son, Harilal, has only recently joined his father's standard. The last move of the government in confining his fragile father and mother for an indefinite stay in jail, was too much for him. So the Gandhi family is once more united in spirit as in the old days in South Africa when the boys hung to the corners of Mrs. Gandhi's saris or ran to Mohandas Gandhi with their broken toys. It is also significant of the standard of this family that not so long ago the Gandhis adopted an outcaste as their only daughter.

Mrs. Gandhi was only a young woman of twenty-seven when the family moved to South Africa. She had few money troubles at first to bother her, for from the very beginning her husband made a more than comfortable salary. This only meagerly educated Indian woman, however, had a hard job before her learning how to keep step with the educational and spiritual advances of her amazing university-bred husband. But she did it . . . and herein lies the majesty of this quiet Indian woman who through love alone bridged the chasm from riches to poverty, from comfort to prison, and kept side by side with Gandhi from the day when he was a wealthy man, and she the hostess in his home, to yesterday when she begged the authorities, with tears in her eyes, to be allowed to go to jail instead of her husband.

While her husband was making his famous march to the sea to make salt in defiance of the government in the spring of 1930, Madame Gandhi was leading an equally valuable but less heralded march. She gathered a group of intelligent Indian women and led them to cut down "toddy" trees—hundreds in a day. Hindus of caste, as well as Moslems, are, as a whole, tee-totallers. This subject of prohibition is often the first and sometimes the last subject on which the two great religionists agree. But the outcaste has always had his "toddy". This he gets from a sweet date palm tree, which he taps as we do the maple tree for maple syrup. The thin agile Indian lad slips up the tree as easily as we could slip down; he scoops out with a crude tool, the spot from which the white sweet syrup is oozing, and just here he hangs a mud bowl to the tree. He leaves the jar there over night or until it is full, and then boils the syrup in vats. It is then poured into huge jars to ripen into the powerful "toddy" which the outcaste has taken through the centuries, but which any caste man or Moslem disdains. The cutting down of the date palm tree was taken up by hordes of parents and women, and by May of that same year twenty-five thousand of the trees had been cut down.

The Gandhis in Africa secured a considerable amount of land and founded what they called the Tolstoy Farm at Johannesburg, and the Phoenix Ashram. It was here, as has been mentioned before, that the whole *Satyagraha,* or passive resistance program began. It was on the Phoenix Farm that Mrs. Fisher and I found Monilal, the image of his mother, still carrying on in 1925. We saw him first out in a shop setting type for "Indian Opinion" whose editorship he had inherited from his father. Soon he was at the typewriter, correcting an English editorial, for it was published in two languages. In those days he was dressed in European clothes and entertained us with Indian food served in good European style. The entrance to the farm was conditioned on "no caste or creed", and this spirit has seeped down to the most impoverished indentured Indian laborer in Africa. When we ventured to talk about caste at Phoenix we were told, "There is no caste or creed division among us here; our teacher, Mahatma, would not allow us to speak the word."

In all these ideals which Gandhi originated many years ago, Madame Gandhi was a cooperator. This Brahman woman, whose husband's annual income ran up into the thousands, would be found cleaning the room of a foreigner, or an Indian outcaste. True, she at first found it difficult to adapt herself to such a rapid change in customs from the Brahman "touch-me-not" attitude to the creed of the passive resister "I am the servant of all." But she loved her husband, and so she learned the ways of the new India. Sometimes he and she would clean and work together, to prove to all their people that reform was in the air, and they were not too proud to lead it.

Gandhi was corresponding with Tolstoy at this time, and he must have realized what the cooperation of his own wife was meaning to this huge experiment, especially in contrast to Tolstoy's experiences. When the aristocratic Tolstoy decided to identify his life with the Russian peasants, he called his wife to him to talk the matter over. The result was that he made out papers, giving all real estate and personal property to his wife and children to hold forever. He had renounced property, but the Countess Tolstoy accepted the gift, and continued her life in the accustomed manner. Madame Gandhi, on the contrary, not only willingly saw her husband's large income going to feed a motley colony; saw it publishing a newspaper, but also herself served caste and outcaste with the same care with which she served her own family.

It took a giant character to do this. No wonder her husband now says that "woman is the incarnation of tolerance" and urges her to take a large place in the new India. For if Gandhi's attitude towards women be changed from that of the old Hindu, it is largely the influence of his wife that has accomplished this. At first, the child of old Hindu customs, he had the belief that it was merely a wife's duty to tolerate every hardship; that she must keep quiet even though she suspected her husband of any crime; but that if a husband suspected the wife, she was ruined; for the law has no redress for her, and no Hindu wife may seek a divorce in a law court. But gradually Gandhi's whole inherited attitude toward women was changed into positive appreciation of them as human beings, rather than as property or playthings. He became willing to throw away his inheritance of male superiority and accept that of a comrade. "THE EQUALITY OF WOMAN" is therefore one of his five powerful points of social reconstruction for all India. No longer will the woman be the husband's bondslave, but his companion and helpmate, "an equal partner in all his joys and sorrows, and AS FREE AS HER HUSBAND TO CHOOSE HER OWN PATH."

Today Gandhi says "Woman is not the weaker sex but the better half of humanity, the nobler of the two, for even today she is the embodiment of sacrifice, silent suffering, humility, faith and knowledge. Woman's intuition has often proved truer than man's arrogant assumption of knowledge."

IN POLITICS

The Indian Woman's Congress in 1929 acted as hostess for the first All Asia Woman's Conference at Lahore. The most recent of these Woman's Assemblies held in Madras in 1932 had as the chief themes, untouchability and home industries . . . two points where the home most vitally touches social life and industry. These women are not only talking reform, they are organizing to see that a gradual process of education in these matters is carried on throughout the country, province by province.

One Provincial Woman's Congress held recently in Bihar, under the Presidency of Mrs. P. K. Sen, went on record: "The Conference approves of co-education in primary schools as well as at University stages, and strongly recommends to parents to send their daughters to the boys' schools or colleges, where there are no educational institutions for girls."

The fearlessness of Mme. Gandhi in all of these reforms in which she has cooperated with her husband, has given the women of the country a sudden forgetfulness of self. For trained intellect, for a knowledge of languages, for parliamentary ability, Kastarbai Gandhi cannot be compared to Sarojini Naidu, or to many of the ruling queens of India. But in courage, in suffering for her country, in sacrifice for the great ideal, she outmatches them all.

When the time came in South Africa in the course of the great non-resistance experiment, when it was rumored that the women from the Phoenix Ashram must perhaps go to jail, Mme. Gandhi felt hurt that her husband had not asked her to go. "If you can endure hardships, and so can my boys, why can I not?" she asked "I am bound to join the struggle" and from that moment to this day she has been a vital part of it. Her husband explained to her that he dare not take the responsibility of asking her, as she might feel it her duty as a wife to comply with his wishes, but that since she had made up her own mind, he could not refuse her. She then, with her children and the three thousand, made the long march from Durban to Pretoria, some six hundred miles to jail.

It is little wonder that Ramdas and Devadas are now in prison, or that Devadas was his father's bodyguard during the trying days of the Round Table Conference in London. After those prison days Mme. Gandhi's health was greatly weakened, and it seemed to many of her friends that she could not live through another campaign. When the struggle was finally over, Kastarbai and her husband sailed for London from South Africa, but Gandhi's illness soon sent them home to the warmer climate of India.

AT HOME

They were at home once more. Mme. Gandhi has not left the country since that time, and the Mahatma, only to attend the London Round Table Conference.

It is curious that Mrs. Gandhi is so little known in the newspapers of the world. Perhaps it is because she goes so quietly in the shadow of her great husband. Still, being the wife of a front page news item around the world must be a difficult rôle to play. This quiet Hindu wife, untutored in the schools, has sipped the milk of great movements. She has lived in the midst of them, and has every time taken a responsible part. She has done a considerable amount of social service work. When Gandhi went to the backward Province of Bihar to fight for the workers on the indigo plantations, and as an aside to put village education and sanitation into their villages, he soon summoned his wife to his aid. She had never been taught in schools, but she began to manage them; and she was shocked to discover the poverty of the thousands of Indian women, who could buy only one piece of cloth. They were so dirty—these village women—and yet when she asked why they did not wash their clothes, she found that they possessed only one sari at a time!

The women, led by Mme. Gandhi, did not stop with destroying the outcaste's "toddy". The white man's liquor has been making inroads among caste people and the formerly strict Moslems. Licenses to sell liquor in the government shops are auctioned off at stated times, and business men come to buy. The women, knowing the time and place, appeared quietly at the auction. Whenever an Indian business man appeared to offer an amount for that particular license, the women would quietly admonish him; would speak to him of his sons and theirs, and of how the danger of liquor was spreading. "What a traitor you would be to so fall into the hands of the foreigner! To betray your holier upbringing!" In many instances, not a license was sold. In the Poona District, in which the government revenue from licenses was three hundred thousand rupees for 1930 (approximately one hundred thousand dollars) the revenue for 1931 had dwindled to two thousand rupees, or roughly seven hundred dollars. The women attacked the sale of liquor at the religious and social *melas*. Usually the expenditure for drink at these festivals runs from five hundred to seven hundred rupees a

© Acme

MADAME GANDHI SHARES HIS SACRIFICE

day. During the last two years it has been cut down to less than ten rupees a day. On the constructive side, the women have urged people at the *melas* to provide free milk for the babies; and the idea has become infectious.

One has only to read from the old laws of The Institutes of Manu, to realize how far the modern reformers have gone, both men and women.

Manu, writing in the year 200 B.C. says:

> "Though destitute of virtue . . . or destitute of good qualities, yet a husband must constantly be worshipped by a faithful wife."

Gandhi says: "Woman will no longer be the husband's bondslave; she shall be as free as her husband to choose her own path."

Manu says: "For women no sacramental rite is performed in the sacred text; women who are destitute of strength and destitute of knowledge of Vedic texts are impure as falsehood itself."

Gandhi says: "Women are the incarnation of tolerance."

It is more important, according to Browning, to know what we are becoming, than what we are. The trend of Indian womanhood is out and up. And active participation in this war is no surprise to those of us who have watched her. Let us look at a living picture. The Indian political Congress of 1925 was held in the City of Cawnpore. The large Pandal or tent which was erected for the meetings, held about five thousand people. It was packed. And in India when a tent is packed, it means that every inch of space is covered. No room is required for chair legs, or even human legs, for the audience sits on them. Shoes are taken off at the entrances, and one slides down the matted aisles, in stocking feet or bare feet, according to one's custom. Hats are the tell-tale badge for the men. Are you a Gandhi-ite? Then you wear a white homespun cap, shaped like an overseas cap. Are you a Parsee? Then you wear a shiny black hat that looks as though it were made of patent leather. Are you a Punjabi? Then you wear a many colored and regal *pugari* (turban). The head gear's the thing in India. Only the Bengali is bareheaded.

Seated on the platform, one could see spread out before him the geographical, political, racial, and religious map of India—on the heads of the audience. But speaking to that audience was a *woman!* An Indian woman elected to the Presidency of that political Congress. It is one thing to have an Elizabeth or a Victoria thrust upon you, but it is quite another to have Indian men, brought up from childhood on the Institutes of Manu, elect a woman to be their presiding officer. The miracle happened, and the miracle was none other than Sarojini Naidu, the poetess.

We Americans are not so far ahead of India. We think it is a great step for President Hoover to have appointed a woman (President Mary Woolley) on the American delegation to the Disarmament Conference at Geneva, yet at the first Round Table Conference in London there were two Indian women members. And at the second Round Table Conference, Sarojini Naidu accompanied Mahatma Gandhi, for consultation and counsel.

SOCIAL RECONSTRUCTION

The stark reality of this movement among Indian women, the immensity of their task trying to change the home customs of three hundred and fifty million people, is almost appalling for an outsider to contemplate. If our women of the present day are proud to be Daughters of the Revolution and Colonial Dames, because their ancestors were made of "the stern stuff of pioneers and democrats" what will the descendants of the present day Indians be shouting? The world outside India knows few of the names of these leaders. But all India knows them.

Take Urmila Devi, for example. Tutored from childhood by Indian and English masters, she is equipped with several languages. She has never travelled from the shores of Hindustan, yet she is at home in international relations. She is a rigid vegetarian and an excellent cook, and has often laughingly wondered whether she could make a living in America, as cook in a vegetarian restaurant! Her program is varied. She has a school for Brahman women in which she teaches them to spin, to read; she is the voluntary manager of a hospital built in memory of her brother, C. R. Das, former mayor of Calcutta. She is an ardent nationalist. During the strenuous days of the last Indian Congress, she cooked every meal that Gandhiji ate. She knew that her food would be appropriately chosen, well cooked and sustaining for him during his heavy program, and she, a Brahman, did this as a matter of course.

Another one of India's pioneer women is Sarala Devi, a niece of the Poet Tagore. She, like Urmila Devi, was trained by tutors, and has no college degree, but she is a woman of marked intellect and talent. She is a musician; she writes in a literary style in several languages. She is an internationalist in every sense of the word; yet there has been one thing that rancored in her mind—the arrogant white man, who stalked through her country, tramping down her culture, and leaving no room at the top for her sons. She once heard a young Britisher, who had just arrived, talking to some friends of hers about his future, as a diplomat. "Now that I am here" he said "the sky's the limit, if I make good." "That is it" she said, "My sons can never say 'The sky's the limit' because every son of India knows that he cannot rise in diplomacy; he cannot rise even in their Army or Navy." She decided to train her two sons for a military life, in the hope that they could get the higher training in some foreign country, and, as she said, "They will be able to speak the military language —the only one the white man really comprehends." A perfectly normal conclusion.

When her sons were in their teens, she employed the best fencing master available. She invited her friends' sons to join the classes, and they all made progress. But when the time came for them to enter college, Sarala Devi met Mahatma Gandhi. And there the story breaks in two in the middle. She sat at his feet for a week. At the end of the week, she offered herself for service to her country. "But" said Mahatmaji "How can you serve my people when there is such a chasm between you and them? The sari that you wear is rich in gold thread; the jewelry is nauseating with its Brahman exclusiveness. My people get five cents a day; what message can such as you have for them?" "And like the rich young man in the New Testament story" she tells of the incident, "I turned empty away. I was the rich young man only a short time however. I looked at my fingers that had painted pictures, written poetry, had played many musical instruments, and I determined to try the spinning. I hid myself for three months; I was such an awkward pupil. But I stuck to it, and after three months I went back to Mahatmaji—dressed in the white khaddar that I myself had woven. I had discarded my foreign silk stockings, and my shoes from London." She looked proudly at her sandaled feet bare of stockings, as she told me this story, and said, "I have never put them on again from that day to this."

Sarala Devi puts her emphasis on social service, and a few years ago presided at the All India Social Workers Congress, when it was held in Calcutta. She is that rare creature, a really big minded woman, and she would find her place near the head of the table in any international Round Table gathering of the World's leading women.

For a thousand years our European ancestors fought their feudal bloody way. A killed B before B could kill A. Often B surprised A and killed him first. Then there was chaos. Even on to the twentieth century we pursued our bloody way, when millions of A killed millions of B. All these centuries one half the world was unheard from. Down through the ages, woman was always the suffering silent partner. The over-lords of the male world—the fighting world—simply commanded. Woman bore the sons, sent them forth, and endured the wars, because she saw there the beauty of character that suffering brought to those who were left. It brought her in touch with the Great Beyond. She was not satisfied, but comforted. Yet always there was this rancor of "Waste! Waste of human life!" And when she became emancipated and intellectually trained, and given a little power, but great influence, woman began to strike a death blow to the killing of both A and B.

The Indian woman in the army of passive resistance wants to end, not only the killing of her own sons, but also those of her enemy.

Indian women have torn off their veils, and rushing out of purdah, have leaped over the thousand years of feudalism, and have entered into *Satyagraha* war against killing. They do not object to the fact that the world calls India feminine. "Those are the qualities we most admire" they say, "and we shall follow our way on this line if it takes a life time and longer."

Will they win? The unbroken record of ages of the past speaks in the Epic of the Mahabharata:

"Patience is vaster and greater than an ocean;
Do naught to others which if done to thee
Would cause thee pain; this is the sum of duty;
Enjoy thou the prosperity of others,
Although thyself unprosperous. Noble men
Take pleasure in their neighbor's happiness.

. . . .

Bear railing words with patience, never meet
An angry man with anger, nor return
Reviling for reviling; smite not him
Who smiteth thee, let thy speech and acts be gentle."

Madame Gandhi and the Indian women who are with her in the jails of India, are the incarnation of these verses which have been sung in every language of India for over two thousand years. They are testing them now in a national struggle.

CHAPTER X

WHAT MAKES INDIA POOR?

"Me the sea captain loved, the River built,
Wealth sought and kings adventured life to hold,
Hail, England! I am Asia . . . power on silt,
Death in my hands, but gold!" [1]

It was gold that England came to India to find; it is gold that keeps England in India. Lord Rothermere, who could hardly be accused of having an Indian bias, has specifically stated that twenty per cent or more of England's national wealth and current income is derived from and depends upon India, and that for England to give up India now would mean national bankruptcy. One can scarcely blame the financial interests of England for frantically trying to ward off such a catastrophe; but in the face of such facts one cannot give full credence to the oft repeated assertion that Britain is in India merely to keep the peace and that Indian security, national and economic, depends upon British rule.

One of the chief arguments advanced against giving India home rule is that she is too poor in national wealth to develop and control her own resources. What made India poor? How did India get her national debt? Is her present government administered as economically as would seem necessary in a country too impoverished to rule herself? If one fifth of every English pound comes out of India, is the British government advancing the cause of English or Indian national wel-

---

[1] Kipling, Rudyard, *Calcutta* in Seven Seas.

fare? These are questions that should be faced squarely and impartially.

ANCIENT INDIA'S WEALTH

A little over four hundred years ago, the wealth of India was so fabulous that it was the talk of the world. Indeed, it was India's very surplus of natural resources and home industries that brought disaster to her door and made jealous fingers itch. It was in search of a short route to the "spices of Ind" that Columbus set sail upon that momentous journey which was to result in the incidental discovery of America. The Pharaohs, those ancient connoisseurs of beauty, used to wrap their mummies in Indian linen, and took the jeweled boxes of ivory, gold and sandal-wood of India as suitable gifts for their gods.

When the East India Company came into India about the time that the American Revolution was sealing the fate of a different kind of Indians, this situation was comparatively unchanged. The most marvelous draperies in the world were still woven in India, materials so sheer and delicate that sometimes a craftsman spent half a year weaving a single bolt. The European markets went so wild over these works of art that they gave them names like modern French perfumes, "Tissues of Evening Dew", "Running Water", "Clouds of Smoke". And the ships of the world stopped at the little village of Calcut to fill their holds with the humbler but scarcely less beautiful calicoes, named for the village from which they came.

Up to the time that the East India Company began by sword and conquest to take over the marketing of these goods, the Indians themselves had carried on a profitable trade for several thousands of years with the outside world. They were a peaceful, beauty loving people, content with small profits and homes such as their fathers had built. There was, indeed, great wealth, and almost fairy-tale display among the native princes of India of jewelry, bars of gold and tangible mountains of wealth. The common people neither wanted nor cared for such riches; they were content to till their small fields and to spend a year if need be, weaving their dreams into a bolt of cloth.

CONQUEST

Into such an industrial gold mine as this the East India Company fought and bought its way. It became so prosperous in its exploitation of Indian jewels, embroideries, linens, prints, spices and copra that for the first hundred years of its existence its dividends to its stockholders never went below one hundred and fifteen per cent, and often stayed in the vicinity of five hundred per cent. It is a matter of record that one consignment of Indian products which cost three hundred and eighty-six thousand pounds delivered in London, sold on the exchange for two million pounds. Gold was also available without even the trouble of mining it. Indian gold and silver representing the savings of centuries was shipped to England with comparatively small compensation to the naïve Indians.

It was therefore not a raw continent that England came in to possess, but a country with manufactures and gold reserves already developed. Besides weaving, there was dyeing in rich colors unknown to the rest of the world, rug making, metal work, damascening of arms, carving, paper making, and the artful cutting of jewels among the craftsmen of early India.

EASY VICTIMS

Moreover India was very easily conquered. She had not been heavily armed since the days of the Mogul Emperors.

Hemmed in by seas and the Himalaya mountains, she had not expected new attacks. A few raiding parties had come down through the Kyber Pass but had been driven back again, and as for a navy, India had no need of that since her wealth brought ships of all nations to her. Bribery had a great deal to do with the success of the East India Company, and many Indians lent themselves to this sort of bargaining. Certain landlords who had the power of rental but not the ownership of vast amounts of land, were told by the foreign merchants that they would be guaranteed the ownership of this land in perpetuity, through the power of the new army if the Indians would come to agreeable terms. Even today the government cannot extricate itself from these early bargains, though it would devoutly like to do so.

These early commercial agreements brought about the setting up of hundreds of small native states. European writers, seeking to show disunion, have put the number of these native states as high as seven hundred. This is not a factual exaggeration, but the vast majority of these are merely the estates of petty landlords, with governmental guarantees, where rents are taxes.

Dacca was the early Lancashire of India. During the year of 1787 at the close of the American Revolution, she exported muslin to England alone to a value of a million and a half pounds. Thirty years later the muslin exports from Dacca to England had dropped to zero. Why? Because of the export and import duties which England had slapped onto Indian goods in order to protect the comparatively crude workmanship that was just springing up in the newly invented machine looms of Lancashire. A duty of sixty-seven per cent was put on Indian goods coming into England, but a duty of only three per cent on British goods coming into India. As the export of manufactured cotton fell off because of the tariff, raw cotton exportation increased enormously. In 1813 there were only nine pounds of raw cotton sent from India to England; in 1838 forty-eight million pounds crossed the seas. These figures tell their own story.

The result of such a high tariff amounted to almost a confiscation of Indian goods. Even British historians have called this "the strangling of a great industry". And since Britain now controlled not only England but India herself, India had no chance to make use of a retaliatory tariff of her own. Dacca became a deserted city. Trees grew up in the houses. Famine and bitter poverty stalked her streets.

The invention of the machine loom, which came about the same time as these early tariffs, would undoubtedly have limited the prosperity of India's hand weaving, eventually, anyway. But normally it would have taken at least a hundred years for Indian hand industry to have been stamped out. Meantime she would have adjusted herself to modern methods. Because of the high value placed upon Indian materials, they would have been in demand in preference to the rough weaving of the early looms for many years, had their price not been so tremendously and suddenly advanced. It was the coincidence of Britain's destruction of India's handloom industries, giving her no machine looms to replace them (which in the paternal governmental form would have been just) that kept India out of the modern march of industrial progress.

With this historical background in view, can any one blame Gandhi as an Indian patriot for identifying military methods with machinery as at enmity with his country? He condemns the present methods of English industrial exploitation of India on the same grounds as he does those of yesterday.

I recall his clear analysis of what he designated as "The Five Major Profits of England." "We in India have too many prophets, but you in the west have too many profits. You speak of 'major and minor prophets' in your own religious history. I want to show you 'the Five Major Profits' of today.

1. You English buy Indian cotton in the field, picked by Indian labor at seven cents a day, through an optional monopoly.
2. This cotton is shipped on British bottoms, a three weeks journey across the Indian ocean, down the Red Sea, across the Mediterranean, through Gibraltar, across the Bay of Biscay and the Atlantic Ocean to London. One hundred per cent profit on this freight is regarded as small.
3. The cotton is turned into cloth in Lancashire. You pay shilling wages instead of Indian pennies to your workers. The English worker not only has the advantage of better wages, but the steel companies of England get the profit of building the factories and machines. Wages; profits; all these are spent in England.
4. The finished product is shipped back to India at European shipping rates, once again on British ships. The captains, officers, sailors of these ships, whose wages must be paid, are English. The only Indians who profit are a few lascars who do the dirty work on the boats for a few cents a day.
5. The cloth is finally sold back to the kings and landlords of India who got the money to buy this expensive cloth out of the poor peasants of India who worked at seven cents a day.

"Does not a government which encourages such a system help to make India poor?" asks Gandhi. "Think what it would mean to the development of Indian industry if all those factories, all those machines, all that cloth had to be made in India! Suppose, as Europe fears, that the Moslems or the Hindus did get exclusive control of the Indian government and monopolies—either one of them—their money would still be spent in India. England is just another sect in control for self-benefit."

GANDHI IN LANCASHIRE

When Gandhi was in England he accepted an invitation to visit Lancashire, and walked through the poverty stricken streets, seeing the effect of Indian boycott of British goods. His face was grave and his heart heavy as he saw the white faced children and stripped homes. Some one said to him, seeing his distress,

"Do you not regret that you have caused all this suffering?"

"It is not I who have caused it: it is war," said Gandhi. "Even a peaceful war must have its victims. I would not bring death or sorrow to an English home, if I could help it. But it is the English man's own policy which has brought this about." He paused and closed his eyes. "I cannot forget the empty streets of Dacca . . . also . . ."

Gandhi is in jail today because he refuses to call off the boycott of British goods which has been so effective as to nearly cripple Lancashire manufacturers. The government has offered to release him if he will rescind this policy. But he cannot. He must be true to his struggle for a self-sufficient India.

"We Indians are denied legislative functions," he once explained to me. "Therefore we cannot fix a tariff to protect ourselves. The boycott is the Indian tariff, imposed not by law but by the will of a whole people. We can not, it appears, obtain legislative power to protect our nation unless we free ourselves by military revolution. This sort of a revolution is contrary to our principles. We will not shoot a man, precipitate him into eternity without giving him a chance to decide what he wants to do about it. We know our passive resistance will cause suffering and death, in both India and England . . . but the Englishman can avoid this if he will."

BONFIRES

But if his country is so poor, demands the onlooker, why does Gandhi sanction the burning of foreign cloth in the Indian streets? Such bonfires satisfy the very human desire of the revolutionists for drama and public protest; they are denied attack upon their prosecutors; they cannot, according to their principles, even resist arrest.

I watched one of these bonfires grow one afternoon in a park in Calcutta. Young college students and instructors came rushing across the grass to the cloth bazaars to demand importantly, "Have you any foreign cloth?"

The cloth merchants grew pale. "We are poor men . . . we cannot afford to let you . . ."

The students interrupted impatiently,

"Bring out what you have. We will pay you for it! We are not thieves. Pile your foreign stuff on the sidewalk."

The merchants obeyed amid growing crowds and excitement.

"We'll give it to you at wholesale"; the merchants grew more patriotic as the fervor grew. "We do not wish to make a cent on this cloth!"

The Moslems, selling meat in the nearby bazaars, called out, "We want a part in this" and threw over coins to pay for more cloth. Joyously the students, helped by a hundred eager hands, carried bolt after bolt of stuff to the centre of the park and piled it up about a bronze statue of a British statesman of uncertain age, whose nose and cocked hat peered out over the curling smoke and noise in mild surprise. There was nothing sinister about the performance. It reminded one more of a Greek fraternity hazing in a midwestern town, than of anything else. The Indians were carefully keeping to Gandhi's counsel about "no bitterness". But they were none the less in earnest . . . in deadly earnest.

These bonfires, whose flames have flickered across the pages of the newspapers of the world serve the same purpose as the electric lights on Broadway . . . they advertise the passive resistance movement. A rebellion which no one knows about has smoldered out. The British government realizes this, hence its close censorship of all news going in and out of India, so that a foreigner who sympathizes with the Indian desire for freedom cannot even have his cablegrams from home delivered. Gandhi knows this need for continual bombarding of public opinion with Indian news.

"Besides," as Gandhi wrote a friend recently, "the British navy shooting at targets here in the harbor burns up more Indian money in one day than all the bonfires of British goods ever kindled."

But Great Britain has been responsible not only for India's industrial downfall, but for India's national indebtedness. How did India get her first national debt? By paying the British for conquering her. Incredible as this may sound, it is nevertheless a historical fact. There came a time in 1858 when the exploitation of India by the East India Company became so flagrant that the counsellors of Queen Victoria said, "We'd better take over India as a crown possession before we lose the whole thing." So the British Crown bought India from this commercial concern whose only right to Indian property was that of aggression . . . and every dollar that England gave for this new possession was charged to India and came out of Indian taxation.

INDIA'S MOUNTING DEBT

Speaking of the abolition of the East India Company, Romish Chandra Dutt, the historian says,

"Their capital was paid off by loans, which were made into an Indian debt, on which interest is paid from Indian taxes. The empire was transferred from the Company to the Crown, but the people of India paid the purchase money. The Indian debt, which was fifty-one million pounds in 1857, rose to ninety-seven million pounds in 1862. Within the forty years of peace which have succeeded, the Indian debt has increased continuously, and now (1901) amounts to two hundred million pounds. The annual 'home charges' remitted out of Indian revenues to Great Britain, have increased to sixteen million pounds."[1]

The "home charges" mentioned meant that India not only had to pay the salaries of the British soldiers who held her, and of the Englishmen who ruled her, but also the salaries of the Secretary for India in the British Cabinet in London and of his staff.

Wingfield-Stratford makes this comment,

> "According to a Parliamentary report in 1892, nearly one-fifth of the whole revenue of India went into the pocket of Europeans, all of whose savings and no small part of whose current expenses went to England and were a continual drain of the resources of a desperately poor community. An unfriendly critic might have said that if England had insisted on bringing her civilization to India, she had made an uncommonly good thing out of the transaction."[2]

In those early days the English argued that the native Indian kings and princes lived in such extravagant style that

---

[1] *The Economic History of India.*

[2] Wingfield-Stratford, Esme. *The History of British Civilization.* (New York, 1930.) p. 1048.

the mass of Indians knew no other kind of authority. Even some of the early missionaries who went out from Europe refused to ask the Indians to dine with them, for they said, "The Indian believes in caste and if we break this down, we will also demolish white prestige." Therefore both government officials and some missionaries lived luxuriously.

Today although protesting that India is too poor to rule herself, the government continues to spend money like water for government housing and living expenses. The new viceregal capital at New Delhi, recently completed, cost over one hundred million dollars. The salary and perquisites of the Viceroy of India make his income three times that of the President of the United States. Even the Governor of Bengal, only one British province, has a home and retinue that would put the White House, with its beautiful stark simplicity, to scorn. Yet America is reckoned the richest country in the world and India the poorest!

Contrast, for example, the arrival of Lord Irwin and of Gandhi, friends though they were, at New Delhi for their conference over the salt tax. Lord Irwin came in on the famous viceregal "White Train", with its whirring fans, its bedrooms, its tiled baths, and luscious food. He stepped out, not on the common concrete pavement of the station, but upon a thick red carpet that swept up the platform, through the waiting room, and out over the pavement to his purring limousine. Everywhere he was surrounded with luxury, with servility, with attention a king might envy.

Gandhi crawled out of a third class railway carriage, full of hot humanity, crying babies, into the midst of his Indian friends, who had been waiting patiently since daybreak. It was raining and the Indians had a car there to drive Gandhi the six miles out to the viceregal palace. But Gandhi said, "No" he would not ride. He needed the exercise after being shut up in the railway carriage so long. But if some one would lend him an umbrella . . .

So this potent ruler walked six miles in the driving rain, carrying victory and a black umbrella. For he came out of the viceregal lodge with most of his claims vindicated.

THE HIGH COST OF GOVERNMENT

"Does the government of India need to be so expensive?" asks Gandhi. "When we rule ourselves the salaries of the government officials will at least benefit India." But the pensions of the British government servants do not stay in India. The young Englishman goes out when he is only about twenty-four years old and joins a government or commercial service, expecting as a matter of course that after twenty years he can go home and enter politics or pleasure, with the support of a pension for life from India. Many retire in their forties with good pensions until they are eighty, if necessary. All this is paid out of Indian taxation and earnings.

"The government has set up various committees to scrutinize public expenditure and recommend economies that could be effected" writes P. O. Phillip from India in February 1932. "These committees are composed mostly of non-officials. One of these committees in its report just published deals with the expenditure incurred by the government of India on the ecclesiastical department. Ever since the establishment of the British government in India the clergymen and bishops of the Anglican church who minister to the spiritual needs of the British civilian and military population in India have been supported from the public revenue. With the Anglican church in India becoming a couple of years ago a church independent of the church in England, provision has been made for supporting the Anglican bishops in India from other than government funds. This change has not yet been fully effected. Meanwhile the chaplains who are attached to the British army in India are paid from Indian revenue, and the Anglican bishops who supervise these chaplains receive also allowances from the government."

The committee mentioned above notes that the government of India at present incurs expenditure on the ecclesiastical department in excess of a million dollars a year. The previous sum was inexcusably burdensome and represented an inconceivable form of exploitation. Imagine taxing Hindus and Moslems to support Christian priests.

RAILROADS

Railroads built by the British which have been of great value in opening up India to modern commerce have paid heavy dividends to London rather than to Delhi. The capital loaned from London was guaranteed a return of high per cent. If this amount was not earned, the difference was to be taken out of Indian taxes. These roads are well planned and managed . . . but the profits go to England, not to the Indians. When America wanted capital to build her railroads across the continent, she borrowed money from England, but she made her own tracks, American engineers laid them, American engines and cars went over them; and when America paid back her borrowed capital she owned her own roads. In India the boom in trade incident to the railroad building all went to England; the steel, the engines, the high salaried labor all came out of England, and were shipped to India in British ships.

The railroads in India have helped enormously in modernization, in breaking down caste by enforced association during public travel, in giving employment to the operating crews. But they have also multiplied British trade. So they can hardly be exhibited as conclusive arguments to prove how much British rule is enriching India. British rule is enriching India only in so far as the enrichment of India brings riches to Britain.

There have been natural causes of poverty in India, which neither Indian nor English have been able to control.

CLIMATE

Climate, that black god that has haunted India from the very beginning, has made the farmer poor. Uncertain rainfall; enervating heat; a swarming populace; refusal to take life. During a famine season I have watched the rats and deer in the Indian fields eating grain which should have gone to satisfy human hunger. The sacredness of animal life has been a costly doctrine.

The cow has been always sacred, but cow-worship is too strong a term, cow-reverence is more accurate. The Indians regard the cow as their greatest friend. She is the living granary, the walking refrigerator of India. It is because these Indian cows can exist on so little water that they are today being crossed with steers on our Texas prairies. I have gone to Indian villages during the dry season, when the rivers are all dried up, when it is necessary to dig deep into the river bottom to find even a shallow well, and have watched the children sitting upon little hillocks, hungrily watching the milking ceremony. You could have hung your hat upon the bony flanks of these cows. But by nibbling tufts of grass and enearthing drops of water they had managed to give a little milk. "Just think . . . just think" chanted these children. "Our other food is gone . . . but still we have curds and cheeses. Truly the cow is the friend of man!"

The reverence of the Indian for the cow may be explained, but the millions of useless animals impoverish the people none the less.

USURY

Another ancient curse of India that makes for poverty is the money lender. There has been no governmental limit set upon the amount of interest a money lender may charge. There are certain events in Hindu life, as in Christian America, such as getting married or buried or having a baby, for which he must have ready cash. In order to get this money to keep up his social and religious standing, the Hindu often sells himself into economic slavery to the money lender. The debts of the father descend to the son, world without end. I once went to a home where a Christian family owed the money lender one hundred dollars. Ten years before the father had borrowed ten dollars. The interest on this loan was a dollar a month; twelve dollars a year on a loan of ten dollars. Sickness and death had so attacked this particular family that by the end of ten years, though they had paid the money lender frequent amounts and suffered ignoble persecution through the years, they still owed ten times the original loan. It was probably this very native system of imposing on Hindu by Hindu which made possible the exploitation of Asia by the European without too much upheaval. India has become more or less inured to economic suffering.

What then makes India poor? Climatic conditions and religious beliefs that cannot be sloughed off in a day; exploitation of the peasant by both the wealthy Indian and the ruling English; a government responsible to London rather than to the Indian people. In identifying himself with the lot of the Indian peasant, Gandhi has arrayed himself against all these evils. His loin cloth is more than clothing: it is a mute dramatic reminder to himself and to the millions of India that he is an Indian peasant by choice, humiliated as they are humiliated; poor as they are poor; fighting to solve India's heavy problems. The spinning wheel is a political symbol of India's poverty.

So Gandhi's spinning wheel whirrs through the London conference, it whirrs at home and in jail . . . it goes with him everywhere . . . to remind this statesman of new India that his people are hungry and naked . . . and that they must find a way to clothe and feed themselves. No one else can or will do it.

CHAPTER XI

THE SPINNING WHEEL

THE flag of new India has upon it a spinning wheel.

"Back to the simple life!" chuckles the western industrialist, settling down among his electric ice boxes, his machine driven looms, and his factories that assemble an automobile and send it rolling gaily over concrete roads in half an hour. "It is foolish to assume that we can chuck a machine age out of the window, just because we haven't quite learned how to steer it properly."

What the westerner forgets is that India does not have to go back to simplicity; she is already there. India is still largely a country of agriculturists. Approximately ninety-five per cent of her three hundred and fifty million people depend for a living upon a small strip of soil a-piece which would be entirely inadequate to produce enough crops for a decent living wage if multiplied five times over. The people live in seven hundred thousand villages; they have never seen a machine in their lives and probably never will . . . except to smell the rank odor of gasoline when the rajah's or the white man's automobile goes bumping madly by. Their wages range from seven to eleven cents a day, during the season of sowing and harvests. During the four or five months when the rice and wheat fields are baked to solid clods, these people have no employment and consequently no wage. Their chief pre-occupation is to get enough food for themselves and for their families, not to satisfy their hunger but to keep alive the embers of life until another harvest.

Among such workers the chance which Gandhi's spinning wheel gives to earn five cents a day extra by their hand weaving is a miracle of good fortune. Not only has the hand weaver a chance to earn an extra pittance during the months of enforced idleness, but by his own hand he can clothe his children. For many a man has had to sell his very loin cloth for a handful of rice.

Moreover, the spinning wheel gives millions of uneducated, economically unproductive village women of India something to do. Except during harvest time, most of these women have a great deal of leisure on their hands. The caste rules and *purdah* regulations, in most cases, prevent them from seeking work in a factory or mine, even if such jobs were available or desirable for them. Yet they are grindingly poor. The question becomes, how can the wives of Indian farmers supplement their husbands' incomes? What cottage industry is suitable?

When Gandhi pulled the spinning wheel out of the Indian attic, so to speak, he answered this question. The English had so effectively strangled Indian home industries seventy-five years before that Gandhi was hard put to it even to find a wheel to try out his idea; but one of his friends scoured the country until a *charka* was unearthed, and the whirr of Gandhi's wheel was echoed soon in a million homes. Here was not only a method of providing work for the largest body of unemployed in the world, but it was also a suitable industry for women at home. Spinning did not require the women to break social or religious regulations; yet it made them at once economically valuable. Two problems—food and clothing—haunt the Indian's dreams. If the farmer husband could solve the first, and his wife the second, the division of labor would be maintained while enhancing the position of women all over India, making them earners as well as housekeepers. And the position of the farmer's whole family would be advanced.

Add to the spinning wheel the boycott of British goods and Gandhi's economic and political program became practical. India formerly imported mill cloth worth about two hundred and fifty million dollars a year, mostly from Lancashire, England. This importing has been tremendously cut. Since Gandhi's last arrest, not a yard of British goods has been sold in the bazaars of Bombay, and similar conditions are rapidly obtaining all over India. Not only does this mean a financial cyclone to the English, but it means the revival of Indian interest in their own industries. They must have cloth to cover their bodies, and if, patriotically, they cannot buy it from England, the only recourse under modern conditions in India is to spin it and weave it themselves. What this means in reviving the Indian spirit of independence cannot be over-estimated.

THE MACHINE AGE

"I have nothing against the machine as such," says Gandhi. That he uses the spinning wheel on his national flag instead of a shock of grain shows that he knows a larger income and a higher economic standard depends upon his climbing out of pure agriculturalism into some sort of an industrial era. The spinning wheel itself is a machine; a primitive machine, to be sure; but it takes tools to make it. Tomorrow the spinning wheel may be followed by the Indian loom. But at present, as Gandhi very well knows, India has not the organized capital to develop over night highly centralized industries. Nevertheless, the advent of the spinning wheel is the first step in the development of India's machine age.

But India's machine age is not to be patterned entirely upon that of the west; it is to have a social emphasis, a human side which western civilization in its haste to coin material comforts and money forgot to take into consideration. Gandhi's almost vitriolic invectives against the machine age are not so much against the machine as against its abuse.

"The spinning wheel is a standing rebuke against the modern rush for piling material comfort upon material comfort and making life, thereby, so complicated that one is deeply unfitted to know not only oneself, but one's God," says this Indian leader. Remember he is talking to a people already deeply religious, more accustomed to discuss the nature of God than the next break in the stock market. "Moreover" continues Gandhi, "the machine has been more bloody than the sword in taking human life, in squeezing out the very essence of good living."

Gandhi has seen not only the mill towns of England and Africa but he knows also the frightful living conditions among the Indian mill workers of Calcutta. For modern Calcutta is far from the old village that wove "the essence of dreams" into its bolts of hand-woven cloth. It is a modern manufacturing city, with a hundred chimneys belching smoke and factories dumping refuse into the Ganges. So many thousands of workers have come to these factories from their native villages that although Calcutta is a Bengali city, fifty per cent of her people speak the northern Hindustani dialect.

Moral conditions which have been carefully regulated for generations in the Indian villages by the committee of elders, become in these seething, heterogeneous industrial cities unspeakably difficult. The chances are that the men have come down from their villages alone, lacking the money to bring their families. They get lonely and go for companionship to the crowds of women who haunt such districts. They learn to drink . . . certain factories pay their wages with so much cash and so much beer . . . the migrants spend more money than they have ever before seen in their lives. The result is that these men go back to their villages, devoured with social diseases, no wealthier than when they came, to find their families destitute, devoid of even the small support the fathers could have given their children if they had stayed at home. The condition of the women and children who come to the industrial areas is even worse. The women live in huts, wear dirty clothes, since they have no adequate facilities for washing, and either go into the mines or mills with babies strapped to their backs, or feed the wailing children opium to keep them asleep outside the walls.

One very hot night in Calcutta, I was once called to visit a Christian family that had come down from its village and got caught on the industrial wheel. I found a mother, father, three children ranging in age from ten to sixteen years, and a baby in arms, living in a tiny hut so close to the railroad track that the very mud floor shivered as the engines roared by. The entire family slept on this mud floor on a pile of rags, their only fuel for cooking, the coal that fell from the trains which haunted their night's rest. This family had come down five hundred miles from the north because of the lure of the "high" wage. The father and mother worked eleven hours a day, and the children fourteen hours a day among spindles so noisy they had to shout to be heard . . . and the vast sum that all five of these people together earned was forty cents a day!

The most pathetic member of this typical industrial family was the baby. It lay there, lolling its heavy head in the midst of heat, about to die because for weeks the mother had given it opium to keep it quiet as it lay in its little basket outside the jute mill where the mother was busy for eleven hours at a stretch. That very year this same jute company had declared a dividend of two hundred per cent to its English and Scotch shareholders.

VILLAGE LIFE

Is it any wonder that Gandhi cries out, "Go back to your villages; go back to your spinning wheels until India can work out a better plan of controlling this vast machine."?

What kind of home did this Calcutta family go back to? They still lived in a hut, but it was a hut with good thick adobe walls and a thatched roof to keep out the sun. There were brass cooking utensils; straw mats covered the floor; the children were dressed in clean white homespun (for there was now plenty of washing water); they no longer toiled fourteen hours a day but were on their way to learn to read and write at the little village mission school. The courtyard outside the mud hut had been swept to immaculate cleanliness by the mother and daughters. To be sure, the mother had now to work in the fields, beside her husband, but the baby slept under the cool shade of a mango tree. The father toiled in his field from sun-up till dark, but at night he joined in the joyous sing-song of his friends in the courtyard. Instead of the roaring of the trains and spindles, there came faintly the hum of his wife's spinning wheel.

The cash income of this family was now only about sixteen cents a day as compared with the forty cents which the entire group had been able to earn in Calcutta: but the father had a share in the grain of the community market and the right to an exchange of goods through the winter. For life in one of these Indian villages, especially when the crops are good, in spite of its poverty, is not to be despised. During the day the Indian is a serious-minded person, intent upon his task. If he ploughs, he ploughs, and if he walks, he walks. He never thinks of going for a stroll for pleasure and laughing and talking as he goes, as the white man does. Why should he, when he has probably already had to walk three miles from his home to his farming and three miles back again?

The silence of village-India is tremendous. Most Indians wear soft leather shoes or sandals, and thousands of the peasants have no shoes at all, but sweep along with a slow, powerful stride, not indolent, but steady. You will pass upon the road ten people, going along in a solemn row, the elder leader with a pack upon his back, the women following with packs upon their heads; no one speaks to the other, but they swing along keeping step, perfectly, walking erect and unweary. One of the most fascinating things in the world is to sit and look out across the fields of India at twilight, and to watch the people coming home along the roadway, or stopping at the community well. Small groups of people, and solitary walkers, meditating, not speaking. India with her burden upon her back, silent through the centuries.

But the small country boy of India has a life that many an American boy might envy, for the Indian boy's chief business is to throw stones and to ride the cows and water buffaloes! He throws the stones to keep the crows away from the crops, and acts as a human fence to keep the cows out of these same fields. He must see that the animals are watered and fed. At night he goes home to listen to his father and mother talk over the gossip of the village or sits, wide-eyed, listening to a peripatetic priest telling exciting stories about Indian heroes, dead and living. Santa Claus and Jack the Giant Killer and David and Goliath speak, all rolled into one. What imagination and gestures these teachers have!

For the Indian is not a mysterious person, concerned chiefly with making snakes dance and picking flower-pots out of the atmosphere, as the romantic writers would have us believe. Even the Maharajahs are often not so ludicrously rich as the moving picture officials portray. "The doors of gold and silver" of which the first British "Tommies" whispered in Mandalay were merely wooden doors covered with gilt. The oriental potentate does not even receive his visitors in bed, sad as it is to thus disappoint public imagination. He may welcome his callers, reclining upon a thick white mat or a beautiful rug, but this is at once his chair and his davenport, his entire furniture. And if he attends to his own business by day, at night the Indian knows how to sing and dance, and how to make the night echo with his weird melancholy music. He can work or play; he simply believes in doing one thing at a time. And doing it with resigned thoroughness.

It is this simple human side of life that Gandhi does not want to exchange for the horrors of industrialized cities. This situation of overcrowding and lack of facilities for good and beautiful living is not exclusive to Indian industrial communities; it is common to the slums of all cities built upon our present industrial civilization. The situation in India is simply a matter of the degree of industrial exploitation, due chiefly to the fact that India has no control of her own government or industries. Our current depression shows conclusively that even wealthy America has not yet learned to conquer the machine; the machine sways us. As Stuart Chase says,

> "From our brains have sprung a billion horses, now running wild and almost certain sooner or later to run amuck. Where are the riders with their whirling ropes; where the light hearted youths to mount, be thrown, and rise to mount again?" [1]

---

[1] Chase, Stuart, *Men and Machines.* (New York, 1929.) p. 348.

Since India has been denied the prosperity of the machine age, by foreign crippling of her industrial development, why should she not also avoid its evils? Why should she not, open eyed, appraise the wrongs of modern industrialism, not become a slave to profit-making and man-breaking, but seek to find a way to keep the human element triumphant over the mechanical? Is not this the cry of all our western economists and social reformers, seeking their way out of the morass into which the world has blundered? Perhaps Gandhi's spinning wheel is not the best way, even for India . . . but who can propose a better way to start?

FORD OR GANDHI

At the close of his book "America Comes of Age" André Siegfried remarks that the world must either line up behind Gandhi or Henry Ford. But are these two men so radically different? Both are trying to find relief from a system which throws men out of work without support or redress, which disrupts families, giving them neither security nor happiness. Whether it is over-production in America that is paralyzing industry or under-production in India, the result is the same. Men who need work no longer have it; poverty, disease, and bewildered unhappiness are abroad. Ford is saying that there must be developed some sort of system whereby the factory and the farm may be coordinated: perhaps it will finally work out so that the worker will spend half his year on his garden or farm and the other half making automobiles and ice boxes, sufficient to meet legitimate public demand. Ford himself is investing his reserves in thousands of acres of farm land, upon the theory, he says, that a man's whole wealth must not be in machines alone but in the soil as well. Gandhi says "Spin and plough! Keep one going when the other is idle." Where is the essential difference? Yet men will probably continue to call Gandhi an impractical mystic and Ford a business genius! The difference in their method of attacking this vital question of unemployment and poverty is largely due to the differing needs and resources of their native countries.

Gandhi has abundant criticism of his spinning wheel even in India. Indian critics call spinning an opiate, not a renovator. It is the symbol of India's poverty, not of her coming prosperity they say. Indian poverty can be cured only by removing foreign rule, and foreign competition, by introducing scientific agriculture, machinery and large-scale production, together with the necessary banking cooperation and tariff protection.

All of these arguments have elements of truth; but they are not immediately possible. Gandhi is practical. He does not say that the spinning wheel will solve all the ills of India. But he is not going to see the Indian farmer starve while waiting for the larger, more ambitious plans to be worked out. Gandhi is certainly doing his best to rid India of foreign rule, and by his boycott of British goods he has built the only effective tariff wall that is now possible. Meanwhile, he says to the idle Indian hands, "Spin".

As Brahman hands and outcaste hands alike take up spinning and weaving a new national consciousness is woven along with the *khaddar* (home-spun cloth). Formerly it was disgraceful for high caste Hindus to perform manual tasks. Today a new understanding of the kinship of all India through the dignity of human toil is evident.

The practicality of this man, whom the world delights to see only through misty glasses, becomes more apparent. This accounts for many of the strange contradictions in his program. For example, Gandhi will not take medicine, believing that, as a general policy, to get close to the sun and the earth is to find the best doctors possible. Yet when it was necessary he went to the hospital for an operation; he has advised others to do so. He explains his attitude towards medicine as not being one of antagonism; he is simply trying to live in the way the peasants must live . . . to work out the best and the most practical methods for them under existing conditions.

"We are attacking the idea of hygiene in India impractically," says Gandhi. "We cannot readily get enough doctors for our hundreds of millions, nor will our people for generations have enough money to pay for medicines. We've got to use simple, easily understandable methods, to get close to the common people and improve their position gradually as best we can. We must educate the women of the villages who have acted as midwives, not by sending them all off for western education, as is impossible, but by training them, where they are, to use more scientific methods."

The system of education he advocates for village people is based upon a knowledge of what they can use from day to day. "Our educational system to be universally helpful must not be based entirely upon books either western or eastern. Our boys and girls must learn from life as well as from books. Let's teach them to plough as well as to read, to understand nature and themselves."

Gandhi's final and most potent argument for the use of the spinning wheel to make India independent of the outside world, is that independence brings a satisfaction, an inner well-being that makes for world peace. "If India takes to the spinning wheel she will contribute to the restriction of armaments and to the peace of the world as no other country ever has. It is reaching out for new markets, grabbing at other peoples' wealth which is the fundamental and underlying reason for all warfare. Therefore if you satisfy your own wants, and do not need to snatch goods from others, you make a substantial contribution to the well-being of the world."

"Your highly mechanized system in the west has not brought you settled prosperity, nor richness of soul, nor world peace, nor cultural poise" Gandhi remarked to me once as we sat upon the white matting of his living-room. I watched the wheel before him go round and round, guided by thin skilful fingers. "England has raised the standard of living not by a marvellous mindedness, but by an industrialization that requires ever enlarging fields of natural deposits to supply her wants. All Europe has done the same. The result is that they have to scour the earth for more resources and rob other people to keep up an artificial standard of living. This means imperialism and war."

Moreover, when forty-two million English can have a high standard of living by this method of exploiting other people, and three hundred and fifty million Indians cannot, such a method is unjust. Machinery, the love of power and more power, once it has gripped men, becomes their master. You make a gun that can kill one person today, and tomorrow you produce a gas that can send thousands into eternity. Both love and common sense demand that we renounce or restrict our machinery and gas manufacture and develop the social sciences. The most important thing in the world, is, after all, man. For God's sake and for man's sake, let's go back to simple living; to an emphasis upon the social and spiritual welfare of man. This is Gandhi's philosophy boiled down. Is it wrong?

CHAPTER XII

HINDU-MOSLEM UNITY

I SAT in a motley crowd, representing nearly all the religions and castes in India. The Mahatma had the floor; calm, poised, reverent, almost ominous. This is what he said:

"Hindus, Moslems, Christians, Parsees, or Sikhs, if we wish to live as one nation, the interest of any one of us must be the interest of all."

This is Gandhi speaking to the Indian nation. He thinks that Hindu-Moslem accord can be reached sufficiently to carry on the affairs of an Indian nation. In 1924 he proved that by his own method of fasting he could bring thousands of Hindu and Moslem leaders to an agreement which has been the basis for further important negotiations. The English government on the other hand, declares emphatically, that should Great Britain withdraw from India, the Hindus and Moslems would be at each other's throats before the English ships got out of the harbor. What is the truth of the situation?

The importance of the conflict between the Moslems and the Hindus has been enormously over-emphasized. In 1929 headlines reporting great Moslem riots were blazoned upon the front pages of the newspapers. Yet when the smoke of passion had cleared away it was discovered that out of three hundred and fifty million people, only three hundred and fifty had been killed during that year as the result of religion disputes.

Much importance has also been attached to the fact that in some instances the Hindus have played musical instruments before the mosques where music is forbidden; and that Moslems have cut off the arms of many of the Hindu idols, thus fermenting trouble, more or less wantonly. Yet in 1929 when I was home from India for a few months I arrived at an American town in time to see an angry mob of whites burn down the frame church where negro Christians had been worshipping, because of a dispute over property. I have never known of a recent similar case in India, where a Moslem crowd actually destroyed a Hindu temple. It was only the comparative weakness of the blacks in America which made it possible for this to happen; which permitted thirty-one lynchings of negroes last year in the United States. May there not possibly be some advantage in the very fact that the Moslem and Hindu factions in India are both sufficiently strong to prevent such unpunished murders.

By way of comparison let me quote from an American resident in the Punjab,

> "I venture to say that annually in Lahore fewer men are killed because they are Hindu or Moslem than in New Orleans or Charleston or what have you, because they are negroes. I suppose in the whole history of Lahore not as many have died for that reason as in the single day of St. Bartholomew's Massacre. One need hardly go into the Crusades.
>
> "The point seems to me to be that India is doing rather well in its efforts to bring to fraternal amity two cultures as different as Islam and Hinduism. There is probably more real reason for friction here than in Alsace and Lorraine, but I wonder what would be revealed by relative figures in lives lost from 1000 to 1932 A.D. in the Punjab as against those among our western European brethren over these two regions from 1870 until the same date?
>
> "It should be remembered that in those same breasts in which

hatred is reputed habitually to dwell, resides probably the most naturally peaceful and friendly heart known to humanity."[1]

HINDU PREPONDERANCE

Approximately seventy-five per cent of India is Hindu, twenty per cent Moslem, and the remaining five per cent divided among Christians, Sikhs, Parsees, and other small sects. Therefore the major problem of India is Hindu, not Moslem. Moreover, the Indian Moslem has had a great deal of his aggressive militarism tempered by many years of living and inter-marrying with the Hindus. In Persia and Arabia and other predominantly Moslem countries, the Moslem is so combatant, dogmatic, and militant that no one else has a chance to argue with him. The Indian Hindu for the most part has not argued with the Moslem; by his very tolerance and his cultured ways of living the Hindu has gradually softened the sharp edge of Mohammedanism. In Bengal, for example, although fifty-five per cent of the population is Moslem, the culture is typically Hindu, as social customs and architecture clearly attest.

The only possible way in which the Hindu could have changed the more violent Moslem temperament is by absorption. For the Moslems are far more of a "chosen people" in their attitude toward the rest of the world than the Jews have ever been. God is supposed to have dictated the Koran to Mohammed, who took it down in a sort of Arabic shorthand which must never be translated. No "jot" or "tittle" may be changed or interpreted. Therefore the orthodox Mohammedan has small idea either of personal or of religious freedom; he must act only as God dictated to Mohammed though he cannot, usually, read the Koran in the original.

---

[1] Bancroft, Frank C., Jr., of Lahore, *New York Times*, January, 1932.

LIBERALIZED MOSLEMS

So liberal is the Indian Mohammedan as compared with his fellow Moslems of other countries, that he believes openly in free-will and in the personal and individual approach to God. There are Indian Moslem scholars who have ventured to translate the Koran and to teach parts of it to the masses. They have even written booklets pointing out contradictions or abrogations in the sacred book, putting commands side by side to show how they oppose each other. This comes from living with their Hindu neighbors, the very nature of whose religion invites tolerance and an exploration of all religious beliefs.

More than once, I "an infidel" have worshipped side by side with Mohammedans, as have other Christians and Hindus. I have gone into the court yards of their mosques and discussed the comparative study of religions with their priests. Often I have been invited to speak in Moslem schools. Once when talking at chapel in a Moslem college, my absorbed interest in what I was saying caused me to innocently lay the New Testament which had been open in my hand upon the embroidered green cloth that covered the sacred Koran itself! Men in old Moslem countries have been murdered for less; but no one said a word of criticism to me. For this was Moslem India.

Culturally, the Hindu was bound to influence Mohammedanism as he has Buddhism, Sikhism, and other cults. Indian Mohammedanism may always maintain its identity as a religion, but it will be a religious and social community within the general cultural fold of Hindu India. This has been so with all religions there.

Religiously, culturally, biologically, through the six thousand years of their existence, the Hindus have never been conquered by another race. What gives the Hindu this terrific tenacity? Chiefly, his theory of Karma and transmigration. This gives the Hindu not only a belief in the dignity of an endless past, but it gives him also a boundless hope for the future. He is never, therefore, swept off his feet. It is possible for him to absorb all religions, for each new religion may be the next step in his development. He says to himself, "Suppose Christianity or Mohammedanism is better than what I now believe. Perhaps this is the next incarnation." And if this theory keeps him open-minded, it also gives him eternal patience. "I've made so many mistakes in this life," Hindus have often sighed to me. "But maybe I'll get a better chance in the next."

The Moslems have succeeded in keeping apart from Hindu life to the degree they have, partly because of being bolstered by the English policy of "divide and rule"; support the minority so that it will feel its oats; struggle against the majority and thus keep the white power as the umpire. The theory of the use of force as a weapon is common to both the Moslem and the European conqueror. The Moslems believe in fighting, killing, controlling. To kill a Christian meant, to the early orthodox Moslem, immediate entrance into Heaven. He used to swoop down upon caravans and convert them at the point of the sword, a method very similar to Christian religious banditry in the Crusades. The Moslems have therefore been able to understand the psychology of the British, French, Spanish, and Portuguese in their conquest of the dark man, and have been useful allies of Europe in Asia and Africa.

TWO TYPES OF CONQUERORS

Yet there was a vast difference in the two conquests of India which have been made by Mohammedanism and the British. In one case the conquerors have been merged into the Indian nation, culturally and by blood alliance; while the white man has kept himself essentially aloof and unchanged. The Mohammedans entered India a thousand years or so ago, swooping down through the mountain passes of the northwest. But it was not altogether by the sword that they gained converts to the Koran; inter-marriage and birth rate helped. Nor was marriage necessary. James Bissett Pratt, in his "India and its Faiths" observes, half caustically, "Mohammedans have never been noted for their sexual purity. They are said to be worse in this respect than their Hindu neighbors, though not so bad, it should be added, as European Christians."

Polygamy and the satisfaction of the sex desire was so characteristic of the Moslem that when the Arabian conquerors swept over India they were careless as to what race of women they took for themselves. The taking of many wives meant a conquest for Islam by child birth as well as by sword evangelization. But the curious result in India was that while the children were taught the Koran, they also were in turn conquered by the Hindu culture that surrounded them. The children of the third and fourth generation, while still Moslems, became essentially Indian in outlook. They had adopted, even at this time, so many elements of Hindu culture and society that the transition today from British to Indian rule will emphasize, in the main, essential cultural similarities rather than insurmountable disparities.

The conquest of India by Britain, on the contrary, while illegal sex unions with Indian women resulted, has not brought inter-marriage as a convention, nor has their progeny been so extensive as in the case of the Moslem-Hindu unions. There are not many more than a quarter of a million Anglo-Indians. This means that the British rule does not even have the indigenous biological strength that the Moslem conquest brought. Mohammedanism in India is essentially Indian: the Briton is still a foreigner down to the last drop of blood in Anglo-Indian veins.

RIOTS MADE TO ORDER

England has always tried to dramatize and emphasize the differences between Moslem and Hindu. She has done this by encouraging that the voting be done by religious groups rather than by territorial constituencies. She has fostered the deepening of creedal differences by refusing to adopt non-sectarian, universal secular education which would cut across religious lines. England has appealed, also, to the naturally militaristic tendencies of the Moslem by encouraging him to ask for equal or even greater representation in government, although the Hindus outnumber the Moslems four to one.

"In the case of many of these disturbances," says the always kindly and careful Gandhi, "we hear of government agents being at the back of them. The allegation, if true, would be painful to me, not surprising." English opinion supports this view.

Ramsay MacDonald writes of the "suspicion that sinister influences have been and are at work on the part of the government: that Mohammedan leaders have been and are inspired by certain British officials, and that these officials, of malice aforethought, sow discord between the Mohammedan and Hindu communities."[1]

Lord Oliver, Secretary of State for India under the first MacDonald government, said: "No one with a close acquaintance with Indian affairs will be prepared to deny that on the whole there is a predominant bias in British officialdom

---

[1] Durant, Will, *The Case for India.* (New York, 1930.) p. 194.

in favor of the Moslem community, partly on the ground of closer sympathy, but more largely as a make-weight against Hindu nationalism."

Yet Hindu-Moslem differences can and will be pushed aside. The Sepoy rebellion in 1857 proved to the horror of the English that both sects could pull together when they felt their mutual sensibilities outraged. The slaughter of the English at the Black Hole of Calcutta would probably never have happened had not the British offended the religious principles of both the Moslems and the Hindus. The rumor went around that the English were greasing their bullets, some with the fat of the cow sacred to the Hindu, and others with the hated pig, unclean for the Moslem. The government denied this rumor . . . but the low-castes knew better, for they had to do the greasing. They told the Sepoys that the Sahibs were lying. "It is either mutiny or damnation, then!" said the Sepoys. So they mutinied, Hindus and Moslems together, in mutual indignation.

It does not condone such religious fanaticism to suggest that the white man learn a lesson from it. India has not changed radically in her psychology since 1857. It was the Sepoy rebellion which killed the East India Company and made Queen Victoria decide that her government must take over the control of the country, if Indian wealth was to be held for England. But the Englishman is slow to learn lessons of history. He still does not see that it was Amritsar where both Moslems and Hindus were slaughtered which killed British imperial rule in India and will eventually bring India to Dominion Status or to full freedom. He fails to realize how much his failure to keep his word to insure the integrity of the Moslem Caliphate drew all India together in mutual protest. It brought the Moslems under the Gandhi standard.

THE KHILAFAT MOVEMENT

The Caliphate, under guarantee of Europe, and of England in particular, had Turkey as its kingdom, and the Caliph, who ruled this area, stood at the head of Mohammedanism as the Pope stands at the centre of Roman Catholicism. What is known as Jazirat-ul-Arab, the area bounded by the Red Sea, the Arabian Sea, the Persian Gulf, and the sacred waters of the Tigris and the Euphrates, therefore became the centre of the Moslem faith. This included the sacred home of Islam at Mecca and all the holy places toward which every Moslem turns many times daily in prayer. Imagine the horror of the Moslem world therefore, when it was learned that according to the treaty of Savres the sacred Moslem kingdom, the Caliphate, was to be broken up and the Caliph virtually imprisoned in his own city.

Gandhi shared the grief of his Moslem friends. He, moreover, felt guilty of having a hand in breaking up the Moslem empire since he had helped England enlist Indian troops for the war . . . "troops which have helped the government to have the very power which is breaking up the Moslem empire of the spirit!" The Moslem troops, true to their native military traditions, had fought bravely and well for England in the World War. Allenby had conquered Palestine with the help of Indian troops. And now this same England which had promised to guarantee the integrity of the Moslem empire, was not only agreeing to the break-up of the Khilafat, but profiting hugely thereby.

With Gandhi the acceptance of a responsibility means action. So he protested at once to the English authorities on behalf of the Moslems who were supposed to be the Hindus' deadly enemies. His protest was of no practical avail in stopping the break-up of the Khilafat, but it proved to the Mohammedans that Gandhi was fair and wise. Once more

Moslems and Hindus drew closer together and began to get a faint conception of the strength that Indian unity might mean.

Gandhi himself not only gained a new sympathy for the Moslems but also began to doubt the justice of English policies in India and in all the east. He was too well educated in world affairs not to see that Irak, the supposedly new country brought into existence by post-war treaty, was a joke, a mere excuse for England to get the freedom of transit in the east which she had wanted. The Kaiser was accused of having started the World War, partly, at least, with his eye upon a Berlin to Bagdad railroad. This was now to be the London to Delhi railroad. Thus Great Britain gained control not only of all the water ways to India, but of the overland routes as well. A complete monopoly. And India had helped England to thus wrap around her the new chains of control. What wonder if both the Moslems' and Hindus' faith in the good-will of the empire began to waver. The Moslems and the great leader of the Hindus, in spite of religious differences, once again saw eye to eye against the white man.

A UNITY CONFERENCE

But such unity was only superficial unless it could be expressed in actual terms of cooperation. In 1924 Gandhi saw that the Indian national movement was proceeding faster than the essential unity of spirit between the Hindu and Mohammedan. "I've got to get these two factions closer together" he decided. "A divided India can never win." So in 1924 Gandhi called a national conference of the leaders of both creeds at Delhi. There were about three thousand Hindus and one thousand Moslems present, all of them men of authority. They met day after day. There were arguments, debates, open disagreements, and once or twice even open fights upon the streets. Gandhi saw they were getting nowhere. So he said,

"I'm leaving you. I'm going out to fast and pray over this matter, and shall not return, nor eat any food, until a united program is adopted. I don't mean that you must give up your religious differences, but you certainly can agree to differ, while resolved to love."

Yet still the disagreements and debates went on. One cannot wipe out in one hour the inbred differences of generations.

Gandhi kept his word. He did not come near the conference again. Day by day he fasted and prayed, and day by day he grew weaker. The government and the people grew worried. "If Gandhi dies there will be rioting." Physicians came and gathered about the mat where he lay, and joined their requests with those of the troubled Moslems and Hindus that Gandhi take some food. But he refused. "When you two get together," he told the frowning factions, "then I will eat, and not before." He fasted for twelve days, taking only liquid foods, and on the thirteenth he decided to drink only water.

Some of the doctors, thinking he might die, put dissolved food into the water. But Gandhi detected the food and spit it out. "You are endeavoring to make me a traitor to my vow" he said, as angry as he ever allowed himself to be. "I will now eschew even water." "But you will die!" cried one of his friends, sobbing. Gandhi looked at him gravely. "You forget, my friend, the power of prayer!"

By the nineteenth day the Moslems and Hindus realized that Gandhi actually meant to die unless they agreed. So they themselves began to pray. A unified program was adopted. A committee was appointed, consisting of two Hindus, two Mohammedans, and one Christian, to lead the two great religions out under one banner of tolerance. They promised to carry this message of unity down to the last Indian village.

Gandhi looked at them from out his thin, wasted face and saw that at last they were in earnest.

"I will eat now" he smilingly replied.

He stood up then, a fragile broken figure, with one arm about the neck of a British friend and the other about the shoulders of a stalwart Hindu. C. F. Andrews, Gandhi's friend and historian, says of that poignant moment in Indian history . . . "He hung there like a broken body upon a Cross. . . ."

If Gandhi proved his willingness to crucify himself for Indian unity, other leaders could not entirely forget. Though there have been disturbances since this time, this memory so crystallized the thought of both the Hindu and Moslem leaders that the back of the opposition was broken. The impetus of their old hates still carried on . . . but there was a new background, a new hope for believing that if Indians wanted it badly enough, national unity was possible.

"Gandhi has many times refused to show rancor against Mohammedans. Once he even called off the entire passive resistance movement because there had been violence between Moslems and Hindus. 'We must learn self-control if we want national control' he told them. The leaders of his passive resistance cause were staggered, but the people understood him and were quieted. On another occasion he showed himself an Indian rather than a rancorous Hindu.

"Shortly after the worst of all riots between Moslems and Hindus, when the Mohammedans of Moplah butchered hundreds of unarmed Hindus and offered their prepuces as a covenant to Allah, these same Moplahs were stricken with famine; whereupon Gandhi collected funds for them from all India, and (with no regard for the best precedents in matters of charity) forwarded every anna, without deduction for 'overhead', to the starving enemy."[1]

MONEY MAKES CONFLICT

Money is one of the chief causes of conflict. The Moslem is not allowed to charge interest on loans to the faithful, so his borrowing is done from the Hindu . . . which often causes bad feeling between lenders and debtors. Moreover, while many Hindus will sell to a Moslem, often they will not buy from him . . . which makes trade difficult for the Moslem business man.

The break-up of the recent London conference has been advanced as a proof that Hindus and Moslems will never agree. This is not necessarily true. In the first place, this conference was not a fair representation of all India, as the Indians were not allowed to select their own delegates. Even Gandhi was sent by the government against his first judgment, and the rest of the delegates were picked more with an eye to their British leanings than to their loyal representation of the entire Indian people. However, to the amazement of the authorities, Gandhi was able to weld and make a national unit of even so widely diverse a group of Indians, for not only is this little man the master of Indian psychology, but even his enemies know that he has no personal axe to grind . . . he has no ulterior motive.

The power of such simplicity in a complex world of bickerings and wire pulling is colossal. Gandhi who went so far as to offer the Moslems a blank check, so to speak, and to tell them to write their own stipulations, might have pulled the conference out of the fire, with the help of Ramsay MacDonald, if it had not been for the sudden upset through

---

[1] Durant, Will, *The Case for India.* (New York, 1930.) p. 62.

British elections, which not only took public attention from the Indian question, but put into power Tories who had no sympathy with MacDonald's policy of meeting the Indians part way in their demands.

TORY TACTICS

The change from a labor government to one predominantly Tory in sympathy tied Ramsay MacDonald's hands. The postponement for three weeks of the Indian conference because of the political elections gave the Indians time to get thoroughly homesick and to descend from the high pitch of Indian national sympathy to which Gandhi had raised them. Some of the Indian rulers were taken out to English homes—flattered and bewildered, till they were lost to India's cause. By the time they were back on Indian soil, most of these deserters came back to the nationalist standard, but the harm had already been done.

To say that these Indian leaders were swayed by the thought of the country in which they were domiciled does not necessarily mean that they were weak men. The easiest thing in the world is to take on the color and attitude of mind of the people among whom you are living. Woodrow Wilson has been quoted as saying that after an American Ambassador has been in London six months he is useless so far as the American point of view is concerned. The same thing is true of ambassadors to Washington and Paris and Madrid. Not only did Myron Herrick take on a French tinge while he was in Paris, but a French ambassador to the United States was recalled because it was said that he had become so pro-American.

INDIGENOUS CONSIDERATIONS

There are certain climatic and cultural facts which enter into the mentality of each major section of mankind, and their influence cannot be ignored, even by visiting aliens. That is why it is such a great mistake for Americans or Asiatics to go to any other country to try to settle the questions that concern their own nations. European conferences are dangerous for aliens, not because European statesmen are so much more clever and scheming than any others, but because they are in their home atmosphere. So long as the League of Nations and the world court meet on European soil, Europe must of necessity dominate the world. If they met in America, America would be dominant . . . witness the dissatisfaction of the public opinion of Europe with what their delegates agreed to at the Washington disarmament conference. It is dangerous to have an important matter settled by a league meeting permanently in any one particular place.

How then are we ever to get together to plan a world society? We ought to decide upon a generation of training in world thought, agreeing not to settle in any single conference a major problem affecting all mankind. Each world conference should have at least three sittings, one in Europe for preliminary discussions, for example; the second in America where new environmental and psychological conditions can be brought to bear upon the subject; and the third in Asia. It is highly probable that the ratio of membership at these conferences should be changed, instead of remaining the same, with the big nations on top and the little nations at the bottom. All this sounds very clumsy and expensive, and slow; but in the long run, we would get a much truer picture of the state of world affairs and of world minds, and therefore progress more rapidly.

Yet this very fact that man is so affected by his environment is one of the greatest hopes for the future, because it means that deep down in human nature there are fundamental affinities, and when we are able to understand, not banish, the special atmosphere which has made each nation what it is, we will develop a world mind. In the same way, the Moslems and Hindus, living together, are slowly but surely building up an Indian consciousness.

CULTURAL AFFINITIES

But what practical proofs have we, aside from theory, that Hindu-Moslem Unity can ever be achieved? Indian unity was achieved in South Africa during the struggle for Indian rights. They were so merged that there was no Hindu, or Moslem, or outcaste, or Christian consciousness among the passive resisters that marched with Gandhi to the Transvaal. If this can be accomplished on a small scale, it can also be done on a larger scale, given sufficient time. Secondly, such unity is daily seen in Indian life. I know hundreds of nominal Moslems who are really half Hindus. They observe caste rules and join in Hindu festivals. For example, in Bengal it is customary to use hundreds of little lights to surround the windows, doors, temples, roofs, at festival time. Many times the Moslems have not only lighted their houses in sympathy with the Hindus, but have helped kindle the very flames about the Hindu idols. Yet an orthodox Moslem of the old school would have knocked off the heads and hands and toes of every idol he could. But this is the new India. Third, the Delhi conference and Gandhi's fasting proved that national unity could come if the Indians only wanted it badly enough. Finally, at the London conference Gandhi produced a practical plan of Hindu-Moslem accord. He was willing that the Moslems should have control of enough votes in all Moslem states, and the Hindus in all predominately Hindu states to swing the elections for the majority; he was even willing that such a measure should be written into a federal

88, Knightsbridge,
LONDON, W.
29th September 1931.

The Right Reverend Bishop Fisher,
c/o "Christian Herald,"
NEW YORK.

Dear Friend,

I was deeply ~~cheered~~ touched by your prayerful greetings. My message to American Christians on World Peace and Disarmament is that Peace and Disarmament are not a matter of reciprocity. When real Peace and Disarmament come, they will be initiated by a strong Nation like America - irrespective of the consent and co-operation of other nations.

An individual or a nation must have faith in one'self and in the protective power of God to find peace in the midst of strife, and to shed all arms by reason of feeling the loving power of God and his protective shield, and I hold such peace to be impossible so long as strong nations do not consider it to be sinful to exploit weak nations.

Yours sincerely,

M.K.Gandhi

GANDHI ON DISARMAMENT

constitution as a compromise, till all India grew more closely together.

In the light of our historic states rights controversy in America, where property rights in slaves and the hatred of race fanned the divisions into violence, and the subsequent peaceful operations of a federal constitution, is it too much to hope that the same kind of human nature will be able to rise above such divisions in India?

CHAPTER XIII

CAN INDIA RULE HERSELF?

"God forbid that we should pass judgment upon a people who framed their laws and institutions prior to our insect origin of yesterday!"

These words of Edmund Burke, spoken a century and a half ago on behalf of India, rolled out across an audience where I sat with a Scotch business man and a British Justice, as joint judge in a declamation contest at one of the Indian colleges a few years ago. Of the three student contestants, one had recited the American Declaration of Independence, and now this one was declaiming Burke with fire and enthusiasm. If there is a more eloquent orator in the world than the Irishman, it is the Bengali. When the contest was over, the judges filed out and with due solemnity cast their votes . . . to discover that each one of us, the Scotchman, the Englishman, and the American, had given first place . . . to Burke!

"Why are you smiling" demanded the English Judge.

"Because you Britishers amuse me," I replied. "Here you are, wild in your denunciation of the 'radical' Indian students who want freedom for India, yet your innate sense of fair play makes you give first place to a British plea for freedom. What makes the Indian radical? British and American doctrines of liberty."

If the white man is to be displaced as ruler in the east, he has only himself to thank. He used his weapon of armed force to conquer the Orient. Yet every ship that carried a general, carried a missionary and an educator also. We brought our ideals along with our guns and now the ideals are well on the way to defeat the guns.

Great Britain persisted doggedly in trying to anglicize the Indian by making the educational system a carbon copy of England's own. This is one great reason why the new India demands liberty as the supreme human possession.

With reference to the effect of the educational system upon the movement toward Indian freedom, Wingfield-Stratford says:

> "The mere fact that the whole bias was towards Anglicization had at last the effect of turning young Indians from their own aristocratic and caste-dominated traditions to half-comprehended ideals of western democracy. It was impossible to introduce the most quick-witted people in the world to such doctrines as 'Taxation without consent is tyranny', 'Redress of grievances must precede supply', and so forth, without the certainty of having them applied in a sense that the teacher might not have bargained for, and when such sentiments were broadcasted as:
>
> 'This England never did, nor never shall
> Lie at the proud feet of a conqueror.'
>
> it was difficult to explain that what was sauce for the English goose might be rank poison for the Indian gander." [1]

The Indians then insist that they are prepared to rule themselves; the Englishman is equally sure that the British government is the only one which can successfully keep the peace among these millions of Hindus and Moslems, and incidentally protect British commercial interests in India. The question to be considered appears to be two-fold. First, what can British rule do for India? Can we guarantee it to be so

---

[1] Wingfield-Stratford, Esme, *The History of British Civilization.* (New York, 1930.) p. 1048.

superior to Indian home rule from an economic and efficiency point of view that it should be maintained at all costs? Second, can India govern herself . . . today? Has she the proper national leadership available and citizenship capacities?

SIX THOUSAND YEARS OF SELF-GOVERNING

India has been a nation for at least six thousand years—how much longer we do not know. But we do know that by the time written history began, India had developed a highly organized social system, a literature, languages, art, music, industrial leadership in hand weaving, and a political system of government in village, city and state which had brought her a high degree of national prosperity. It was this very wealth of civilized India that brought the strong arm of Europe to her door. She was a rich prize, which acquisitive Europe coveted.

Great Britain has been in India a couple of centuries, and what do we find today? Sharp dissension between Hindu and Moslem, almost unbelievable poverty among the peasants, a great national debt which began with the advent of the English to Indian shores and has increased three-fold although India herself has had no external wars: industrial desolation. It is possible that the invention of the machine loom might have changed the industrial character of India even had the British not been there to slap on high tariffs on Indian exported goods; but in the ordinary course of events, might not the Indian industries have been expected to have developed at least as much as those of China and Japan? Yet while in 1850 to say a piece of goods was "made in India" was as much of a world recommendation as to say of modern linen that it is "made in Ireland" (the Indian trademark was one of excellence of workmanship) today there is practically nothing woven in India except the coarse homespun which the busy spinning wheel of Gandhi and his followers have produced.

If we had the amount of unrest in America today that India has; if we could keep the government functioning only by detaining some twenty-seven thousand of our leading citizens in jail; if we were governing no longer by legislative power but by military ordinance, would we consider the party in power such a miracle of efficiency? Upon what basis, then, do we assume that British rule in India is a success?

It has been argued that without British control, railroads, modern science, hygiene would be unheard of in India today. Yet might not India have progressed, along with the rest of the world, if England had stayed in her "tight little island"? It is only during the past one hundred years that railroads, electric lights, antisepsis, machine weaving, automobiles, representative forms of government on a large scale, all the vast, chaotic, complicated programs of the modern machine age have developed in any country. India would certainly not have been the only country in the world to remain immune to all progress. It must be remembered, also, that every advance in transportation, every attack upon disease in India (of which there have been few enough) has been paid for out of Indian taxation. Not a penny has come from British pockets. The Indians have paid and paid well for every advance that may have come to them through British rule. And if the money for governing India comes from Indian taxation today under British rule, is there any reasonable basis for saying India is too poor for self-rule?

THE RIGHTS OF THE RULED

In the old days, the Indians ran their own government, their own industries from top to bottom. Now the Indian is permitted only a place of secondary control. The army officers, the heads of police, the governors of the provinces, the magistrates who decide all questions of dispute between Indians and English are all British. Formerly the British magistrates were held in high respect, but since purely political differences have caused Indians of standing to be put in jail by the thousands, it becomes obvious even to the outsider, that if England is in India for India's good, she is also there for England's good. Even her value as an umpire between Hindu and Moslem has been voided by her recent attitude. An American observer, Bishop Francis J. McConnell, has remarked recently,

"An umpire's value is gone as soon as one or both sides lose confidence in the umpire. All Britain's prestige as arbiter and umpire is gone, at least for the present. It has been the rightful boast of Britain that her courts in India have had the respect of India and the world. All that is gone. The sentencing and imprisonment of independence advocates finished that. There were in jail on December 1, 1930, twenty-seven thousand six hundred political prisoners. Judged by the material outcome in preventing disturbance and bloodshed Britain's policy was, I suppose, justifiable; but it played havoc with British prestige. It was taken to mean that Britain could rule India only by keeping the best brains and character of India in jail."[1]

As these pages go to press, a cabled report from the experienced American newspaper correspondent, Karl H. von Wiegand, says:

> "I have just traveled through India from the extreme southern part to Bombay and Allahabad in the North, more than 1,500 miles.
>
> "Talks with members of almost every class of Indians quickly

---

[1] *The Christian Century*, 1931.

reveal that feeling—even hatred—against the British, is intensifying. The current is steadily running deeper.

"British of long residence in India frankly admitted that they fear a big explosion sooner or later. Some even touched guardedly on the 'nightmare of massacre.'

"Viceroy the Earl of Willingdon, with the approval of the British Government and British Parliament in London, has set in motion a gigantic police apparatus of drastic suppression of civil rights, free speech and freedom of assembly, such as the world has not seen in many years excepting in Russia and in Italy. . . .

"Two years at hard labor are given for not leaving your home town when so ordered by police; for flying the Nationalist flag of India; for saluting that flag; for observing *hartal,* that is, closing your business as a protest against the imprisonment of Gandhi; for peaceful demonstrations on the street; for making speeches urging the freedom of India. . . .

"The attempt made to create the impression that Gandhi's influence is on the wane, that he is losing his hold on the imagination of the people of India, is utterly misleading. . . . One wonders whether the British are misleading the world as to the true situation or are deceived themselves." [1]

The major ends accomplished by any good government are six.

1. Guarantee of life and property.
2. Lifting the people by every legitimate means out of poverty to reasonable comfort.
3. Giving universal education.
4. Producing self-respect, self-reliance among its citizens.
5. Encouraging the peaceful pursuit of cultural and social ends.
6. Setting each generation a little ahead of the last.

The British government in India can be said to have been only relatively successful in these things. Life and property certainly are not safe when a man can be clapped into prison

[1] *Time*, New York, April 4, 1932.

without trial and his possessions confiscated by a foreign power merely because of his political beliefs. When a country is as poor as India is today with an average wage of only eleven cents a day, and still England confesses that the fifth part of every English pound comes out of India, British rule can hardly be said to be adding primarily to Indian wealth or comfort. There is, moreover, no system of universal education in British provinces in India, although native rulers of certain native states have introduced compulsory primary education.

Both the educational and political policy of the British has been to continue to set the Moslem against the Hindu. The antagonism between creeds was there, but it has been emphasized by being drawn into modern politics. The same thing happened in Europe during the middle ages; it was political ends that made more bitter the conflict between Catholic and Protestant. This system has worked equally well between Moslem and Hindu.

The British government has not hesitated to stamp as rebellious and "Bolshevik" even purely religious movements among the Moslems. The "red shirts" which the government gives the impression throughout the world is a communistic organization is merely a Moslem temperance society. Their shirts are wine color but the wearers are not in sympathy with the Bolsheviki. They are pious Moslems, who call themselves "Servants of God." The Moslem religion forbids the use of wine, and they object to the British government's policy of encouraging the sale of liquor to the natives for the sake of revenue—a policy that has long been deplored by Gandhi and all patriotic Indians.

Certainly India's indigenous cultural ends can hardly be said to have been set ahead as they should have been when not only political nationalist teaching but even Indian history and art are discouraged in schools having government backing. "The vice-chancellor of one of the greatest universities told me in confidence that he was in daily fear lest his grant be withdrawn because of the manifest nationalist sentiment among the students of the university," said Francis J. McConnell again, in the "Christian Century". "Now understand, dear reader, the educational money is raised from the Indians, and English authorities have had power to withhold it from institutions critical of Britain's rule. Let the present movement toward self-determination be stopped and the English control of education in India will be, and will have to be, part of the defenses of the empire. To take away from a nation the control over its own schools—schools for which it is itself paying—is an intellectual tyranny of the first order. It is impossible to have any worth-while intellectual atmosphere, except that of revolt, in an intellectual system in such a plight."

IMPERIALISTIC FALLACIES

Leaving out, however, economic and governmental issues, excluding England and India as the interested parties for the moment, and looking at the situation merely from the point of view of national morale, can any nation . . . France, Japan, America . . . give to any other nation an unbiased government? One that is really beneficial to the subject nation? The paternal government may be efficient because it does not have to wait for democratic votes, but it encourages a "slave mentality", a lack of self-reliance, a national fear of authority. Especially is this true when a nordic race, committed to the power of the sword, conquers a quiet, cultured, unaggressive people.

It is self-evident that no nation can be great and be ruled by another. Vigorous Europe is the result of a constant fighting for freedom. Through the feudal system Europe has fought her way out to stand upon her own feet. Even America, three thousand miles away from the mother countries, found independence necessary for a self-respecting national existence. In the Orient, Japan and China have the chance to develop a much more virile national character than does India. Why? Because in spite of internal dissension, Japan and China have been their own rulers. Their systems of education were based upon their own classics, as well as upon western culture which had seeped in.

India's national genius for self-expression has been smothered; first, because the nordic took advantage of the Indian's preference for culture and peace rather than the sword; second, because India's very wealth made her the first prey of the bold conquistadores and commercial pirates of Europe. By the time Japan and China came upon the world horizon as possible booty, sufficient jealousy had developed between the European nations to keep each country from allowing the other to swallow Japan or China at one gulp as England had India.

It is a strange irony of fate that the Englishman's very contempt for this "slave mentality" in India, this passivity which he himself had helped to create, is making for the present instability of his empire. He seems never to have dreamed that India could assimilate individualistic, democratic ideals of freedom.

The present British administration in India refuses to translate the handwriting on the wall; to admit that the day of armed violence as a method of maintaining white prestige in the east is gone forever. Says the new Viceroy Willingdon, "I and my government are determined to use to the full the resources of the State in fighting, and defeating a movement which would otherwise remain a perpetual menace to orderly government."

Such a remark is strangely reminiscent. The "ich und Gott" policy of the World War has not resulted in any great advantage either to the victors or to the conquered. The "I and my government" policy does not seem to be working any better in India.

TURNING THE TABLES

In order to understand the increasingly vocal protest of the oriental against the white man running his affairs by force, it is necessary to put out of our minds the supposition that our civilization is intrinsically superior to that of the east; to think of the Japanese, the Indian, the Chinese, merely as other human beings.

With this premise in mind, imagine how the United States would feel if Japanese troops should land simultaneously at San Francisco, San Diego, and Vancouver, and march victoriously eastward to the Rockies. Then sweep on across the country to New York and Washington, grab our government machine and our gold. They have "got" us by right of superior power. The soldiers, being all Buddhists, have a right to chaplains and therefore to temples which the Japanese build. The Japanese brand of education must be set up in order that our children may develop a Japanese mentality. So these rulers say to us, "We are providing you teachers. We are giving you an efficient government. Your trains run on time, and your letters are delivered. Our government is keeping down riots and rebellion. This is all for your own good; so you must pay for it." We are a conquered people. We have the gold. So we pay.

Then the Buddhist missionary societies say to us graciously, "We'll pay the travelling expenses of missionaries to convert you to the great truths of Buddha. But we expect the American Buddhist church eventually to become self-supporting . . . though we will hold the property."

Then suppose, our Japanese conquerors should go down south and see the blacks not allowed to vote, being strung up in lynchings, and say, "See here. This won't do. You white Brahmans must not be allowed to ride on the necks of the blacks. You must have equality; must attend the same schools; break down your caste system. Intermarry!" Would we resent this program? Yet that is exactly what the Englishman has done in India; what the white power tried to do all over Asia.

But to say that Britain has failed to give India an adequate government does not answer the question,— "Can India rule herself?" . . . now . . . today . . . not one hundred and fifty years ago.

India was never more fitted to rule herself than she is in 1932. She now has more living college graduates than England: she has more students pursuing university education than there are in all the British Isles. Nor is this education of the young Indian of a lower standard than that of the modern English student, for Indian college degrees are based upon the Cambridge standard. In many cases the very examination papers for degrees are corrected at Cambridge. Text books, lectures, examinations, are all in the English language. Even disregarding the hundreds of Indians who have been graduated from English, American, German, and other European countries, the dyed-in-the-wool, made-in-India young intellectuals might be expected to hold their own with English government servants. And though the much heralded illiteracy is appalling, India has more millions of literates than the total population of Great Britain! These millions of literates might manifestly furnish leaders.

There are plenty of experienced men to form an Indian cabinet. Gandhi is as practised and practical a diplomat as there is in Europe today. His knowledge of law, both Indian and international, his fearlessness, his almost uncanny ability to study and make use of the psychology of nations, both white and brown, would make him an ideal premier for India.

GANDHI'S POLITICAL PLATFORM

Compare Gandhi's reform platform with that of political parties in any European country. What does he want?

1. Protective measures for home industries.
2. Stabilized rupee.
3. The present land tax cut in half. (This measure is not aimed at the British solely but against his own caste of landlords and business men who have taken advantage of the Indian peasant.)
4. Salt tax abolished. (Salt is a necessity for even the very poor.)
5. Salaries lowered all along the line in order to help balance India's national governmental budget.
6. Political prisoners released.
7. Prohibition not only of liquor but of opium sale.
8. The income of coastal shipping to go to the Indian government.
9. Military expenditures cut in half.
10. Educational expenditures raised rapidly, tending toward a non-sectarian system of universal education.

Is this the program of a mystic, or that of a trained student of government? Gandhi has the right mixture of poise, worldly wisdom and humor to act as the first head of the Indian state. When he went to England to represent his country, he was never at a loss. Many Englishmen with whom he had to deal at the Round Table conference expected him to be a typical oriental with small idea of time and much of his own importance. They found the Indian as punctual as a western business man at his committee meetings. Indeed, so prompt was he, that often he had to sit and wait for his fellow committee members. One day when thus waiting, a newspaper artist asked the privilege of sketching him.

"How long do you think it will be," asked the newspaper man, drawing busily, "before you can convince England that India should have her freedom?"

Gandhi reached over and snatched the half finished sketch from the artist, and gravely added to his shaven chin a beard of very long whiskers.

"That long" said Gandhi, with a twinkle in his eye.

I ought to have had a whole chapter on Gandhi's sense of humor, including his capacity to laugh at himself and to poke sharp fun at his friends. These unexpected jokes make him intensely human. Some of my friends, handling the truth very carelessly, reported that when they asked him why it was that he observed every Monday as a day of silence, he replied, "Fred Fisher came over to see me early one Monday morning and started talking. He kept it going all day and I could not get a word in edgewise. It seemed such a pleasant experience not to have to talk at all for a whole day that I suddenly decided to adopt it as a habit."

A recent personal illustration of this wit may bear repeating. After Gandhi had hung up the receiver following our trans-Atlantic telephone conversation, a newspaper reporter told him that the call must have cost me as much as a hundred and fifty dollars, whereupon Gandhi chuckled and

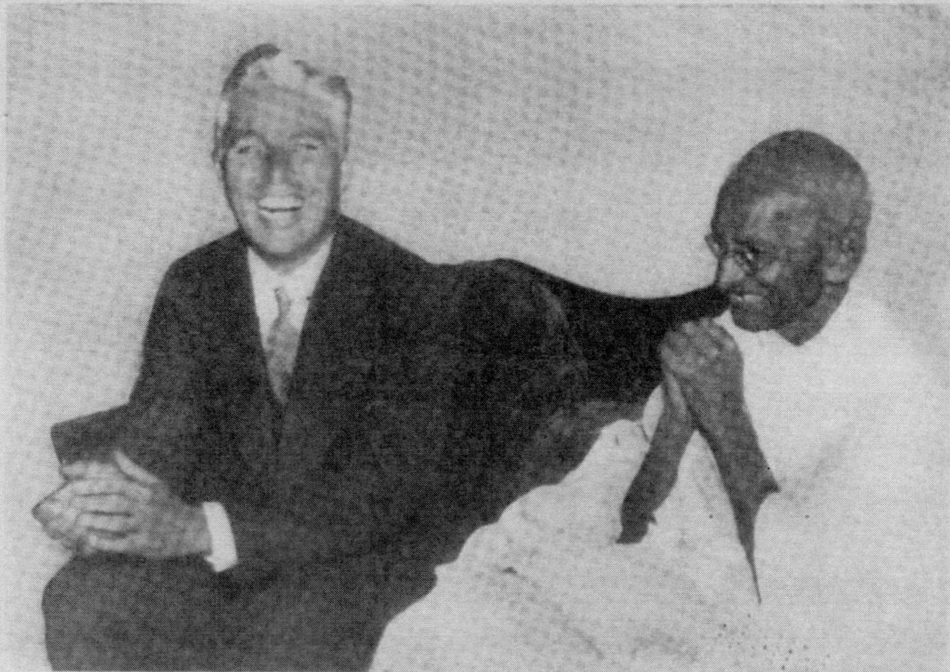

HE MAKES CHARLIE CHAPLIN LAUGH

said, "Wouldn't you think a Bishop would know better than to spend that much money just to talk to me?"

A sense of humor is a very valuable possession in a reformer. Sometimes Gandhi has used a smile to sharpen the point of a political arrow. Rumor has it that one day shortly after he had persuaded the government to legalize his contraband salt, he was having a conference with his friendly enemy, Lord Irwin. The Viceroy being a typical Englishman, wanted his tea at four o'clock and invited Gandhi to join him.

"Thank you," said the little patriot, unwrapping a paper parcel, "I'll put some of this legalized salt into my tea to remind us of the famous Boston tea party."

When Gandhi went to Buckingham Palace to see the King, he wore his usual dhoti and shawl without embarrassment and came away, an amused twinkle in his eye, remarking, "The King had enough on for both of us!" This man who has both humor and poise, mingled with an understanding of national psychologies and an idealism that he dares to practise every day, could well be trusted as the premier of a great nation.

FORMING AN INDIAN CABINET

Nor would Gandhi have great difficulty in finding ministers for his Indian cabinet. Pandit Madan Mohan Malaviya, the president of Benares university, who has had much the same training that Woodrow Wilson had, could easily act as Indian foreign minister. J. N. Tata, the powerful and financially successful business man at the head of India's great steel works, could be India's Mellon. K. Natarajan, editor of the "Indian Social Reformer" in Bombay, whose pen is so trenchant that even the Mahatma listens when he speaks, might prove a competent balance wheel for political enthusiasms. There are hundreds of Indian doctors and surgeons who could head a national department of hygiene and health. City wide campaigns for better babies, clean milk, and other public health measures have already been carried on by Indians themselves; it would be only a step to make such a health campaign national. Certainly public health conditions could hardly be worse than they are today under British rule. Might not an Indian scientist, such as Sir J. C. Bose, find means of appealing to Indian public opinion in a way impossible to an outsider?

Marked executive prowess has been shown for years by heads of many native states, all of which ability could be put at the disposal of a united India. The Maharajah of Bikanir, ruling a modern state, has built canals for irrigation, opening up great areas of formerly waste land, and inviting even outcastes to come in and settle and build homes. He has also inaugurated a most efficient system of primary public education among his people. His attitude towards the education of women is strikingly modern.

The Nizam of Hyderabad, probably the richest man in the world, has installed a state railway and a system of primary education, well organized and scientific. The international university of Rabindranath Tagore at Bolpur is second to none in cultural methods. Would not any of these men qualify to help India rule herself?

Successful government does not depend only upon brilliant and competent rulers at the top, but upon a solid basis of self control in the community and the home . . . as our flouting of law in America has shown only too plainly. No race on earth has more self control, more loyalty to principles and moral codes than have the village people of India. Their village government, evolved through thousands of years, is the very form of commission government which our modern western cities are finding most efficient. The members of the board of select men in an Indian village, rule the town much as in old New England. The oldest man on the board serves as chairman, ensuring a conservative leadership. The marriage licenses, caste codes, quarrels between neighbors, violation of social ethics come before this calm village tribunal which has the power of excommunication, fines and other effective discipline. The result is that a steady order is maintained in an Indian village.

I have slept on the edge of Indian towns, on open verandas, with clothing and money unprotected, and have never lost even a penny. I have put up in village hotels where no room in the house can be locked, leaving all my valuables strewn around and yet have come back to find everything untouched. With a social consciousness and a local government like this at the bottom, it is fairly easy to rule at the top.

It is a significant proof of the efficacy of this native rule that the British have thought it best to uphold these local codes rather than to try to introduce their own legal procedure. It is this very law abiding character that has made it possible for a few thousand white men to govern the millions of brown men in India.

ENFRANCHISING UNTOUCHABLES

"But," asks some one, "what about the outcastes? Do they not present an insuperable problem to self government?" The Hindus have recognized the fact that the outcaste is a problem . . . but not an insuperable one. The outcaste in India bears about the same relation numerically to the whole Hindu population as does the negro to the white in the United States, and has about the same social significance. The slums in which the outcaste lives are no greater in proportion than the slums of our own great cities.

A highly educated man, Dr. Bhim Rao Ramji Ambedkar, represented the untouchables at the London Conference, and he stood side by side with Gandhi in his stand for Indian home rule. There are Hindu states like Baroda, where educated outcaste men become ministers of education, college presidents, and high school principals. In Tagore's school the outcaste and high caste boys study side by side out of the same books, play marbles together, and eat together. The problem is there, for India to solve, but it can be solved more easily by national Indians than by any outside influence.

Gandhi has long been arrayed on the side of the outcastes, and has fought for their place in Indian society along with all other castes.

"I would rather be torn to pieces than to disown my brothers of the suppressed classes," says Gandhi. "I do not want to be re-born, but if I have to be re-born, I should be untouchable so that I may share their sorrows, sufferings and affronts and endeavor to free them from their miserable condition."

He insists also that any disciples, or even listeners of his shall treat the untouchables as brothers.

"In the course of our march to the sea we were once confronted with a unique situation" relates one of Gandhi's companions. "The 'better elements' of orthodox Hinduism of a small village erected a fine platform for Gandhi facing the main part of the audience. The 'untouchables' were seated at a safe distance—on a hill farther away to the right. Upon learning of this extraordinary arrangement of discrimination at a function held in his honor, Mahatma Gandhi asked us, his companions, seventy odd, to go to the hill and sit along with the 'untouchables'. Then stepping on the dais, the leader gave a challenge to the 'better elements' of the community, saying that either the 'untouchable' brothers and sisters as well as his companions who were the guests of the village should all be permitted to mingle freely with the main audience or he would be compelled to go to the hill himself and 'address you all from the midst of my "untouchable" brothers and sisters.' One by one the elders of the village got up and apologized for the arrangements which they said had been made to avert possible resentment in the community: they now welcomed the 'untouchables' into their midst. Gandhi exacted a promise from them that on the morrow no violence would be done to any of the 'untouchables' for their 'audacity' to mingle with the high-caste."[1]

The fact is, Indian leaders and the wealthy and influential families are getting under the social and economic problems of India as never before. They are supporting the movement for passive resistance and Indian freedom just as our wealthy Americans are bolstering up the United States during our period of depression. There are the same organizations, the same committees of influential men and women working for the public good as there are in Boston, New York, or Los Angeles. I have seen as much public spirit and generosity among the peoples of Calcutta as in the university city of Ann Arbor, Michigan. And there is about the same relative public poverty to be taken care of, for the joint family system in India means that each family takes care of its most remote relations, in so far as possible.

Is such an India able to rule herself?

SHOULD INDIA DIVIDE LIKE EUROPE?

Suppose however, for the sake of argument, that home rule would mean the break-up of the country into a number of independent states. India, with the same constituency that

---

[1] Muzumdar, Haridas T. *India's Non-Violent Revolution.* (New York, 1930.)

she has now, was able to worry along as a nation for six thousand years: but suppose the withdrawal of British troops would mean division into states. What of it? "Self determination" meant the tearing up of old boundaries after the world-war: but Europe seems to be able to worry along even with an independent Poland and Czechoslovakia. The day after the treaty of Versailles was signed Europe had twenty-seven political entities instead of the twenty-one she had had the night before.

Bengal has a cultural background very different from the rest of India . . . as different in language and content as France is from Germany. And there are ten million more people who speak Bengali than the entire population of France. Suppose Bengal did set up for herself? Suppose certain Moslem states or Hindu states did draw their own boundaries? What is to prevent them, nevertheless, from having a federal Indian constitution, granting states rights and federal responsibilities, patterned after our own constitution? And can any one conceive of the Hindus and the Moslems flying at each other's throats with more ferocity than the Catholics and Protestants of Europe have done in the past? If territorial division, as in disunited Europe, were necessary, and if self government for India could be achieved in no other way, I would say let that be the road. Unity is desirable, but not at the cost of robust, progressive, independent character.

But a break-up of India would not come for two reasons. 1. The closely knit national consciousness of India which has kept her a cultural unit for three thousand years even under foreign control and provocation. 2. India now in the passive resistance movement is trained as never before in national self control and sacrificial cooperation.

India can rule herself . . . now.

CHAPTER XIV

A COOPERATIVE WORLD

The statue of a fat little lady in hoop skirts presides over the parks of the east. In India, in Malaya, in Africa, down where there is nothing but a desert, stands Victoria in metal majesty. On her head she wears a crown surmounted with a cross and in her hand is a sphere of the world . . . with a cross above it. Sometimes there is a sword in her other hand, but often it is concealed by her iron petticoats. An imperial paradox. Proclaiming piety, and dependent upon a gun. Below each of these statues should be mounted the "consistent war prayer" of Mark Twain who said that this must be published only after his death, for only dead men can tell the whole truth.

> "O Lord our God, help us to tear their soldiers to bloody shreds with our shells; help us to cover their smiling fields with the pale forms of their patriot dead; help us to drown the thunder of the guns with the cries of the wounded, writhing in pain; help us to lay waste their humble homes with a hurricane of fire; help us to wring the hearts of their unoffending widows with unavailing grief; help us to turn them out roofless, with their little children to wander unbefriended through wastes of their desolated lands in rags and hunger and thirst, sport of the sun flames in summer and the icy winds of winter, broken in spirit, worn with travail, imploring Thee for the refuge of the grave and denied it—for our sakes, who adore Thee, Lord, blast their hopes, blight their lives, protract their bitter pilgrimage, make heavy their steps, water their way with tears, stain the white

snow with the blood of their wounded feet! We ask of One who is the spirit of love and who is the ever faithful refuge and friend of all that are sore beset and seek his aid with humble and contrite hearts. Grant our prayer, O Lord, and Thine shall be the praise and honor and glory now and ever. Amen."

Not content with urging his own superiority over the dark man of the east, the white man has called to witness, God himself. In retrospect, it seems almost impossible to believe the colossal egotism of the white conqueror. Take Cecil Rhodes, for example, the voice of British Imperial policy, who not only opened up Africa, her minerals, her wealth, her manpower, to the hand of the Englishman, but who also tried to foster a closer union among all English speaking peoples by his Rhodes scholarships.

Basil Williams, in his life of Rhodes, in spite of every attempt to excuse the overweening ambition of this Anglo-Saxon imperialist, says that Rhodes came to the following conclusions, "God was obviously trying to produce a type of humanity most fitted to bring peace, liberty and justice to the world and to make that type predominant. Only one race approached God's ideal type—His own Anglo-Saxon race. God's purpose, then, was to make the Anglo-Saxon predominant and the best way to help on God's work and fulfill His purpose in the world was to contribute to the predominance of the Anglo-Saxon race and so bring nearer the reign of justice, liberty, and peace."

How was this different from the Kaiser's "Deutschland über alles"? Practically every national anthem in the world has as its theme, spoken or implied, a similar declaration of superiority; it is the very pap upon which our children have been fed. An actual paragraph from the will which Cecil Rhodes drew up at Kimberly in 1877, reads like a declaration of British inalienable rights. In this will he wanted to leave his money to a great secret society to be endowed, with the following object:

> "The extension of British rule throughout the world, the colonization by British subjects of all lands where the means of livelihood were attainable by energy, labor and enterprise, and especially the occupation by British settlers of the entire continent of Africa, the Holy Land, the valley of the Euphrates, the Islands of Cyprus and Candia, the whole of South America, the Islands of the Pacific not heretofore possessed by Great Britain, the whole of the Malay Archipelago, the seaboard of China and Japan, the ultimate recovery of the United States of America as an integral part of the British Empire." [1]

These are not the ravings of a modern biographer intent upon "debunking" a great man, but a faithful transcript of the words of one of the leaders of European colonial expansion . . . who voiced the conceit of all the white nations, as illustrated by their actions at that time. It is entirely encouraging to note the progress of world thought which today finds such an outspoken assumption of the God-given superiority of the white man as something to be soft-pedaled. Yet like a voice from the dead Winston Churchill's addresses in America this year 1932 breathe exactly the spirit of Cecil Rhodes' outgrown bombast.

PRESTIGE AND PROFIT

What were the two big ideas in the colonial expansion of Europe, which was practically coincident with the period of its industrial development? Prestige and profit. The trader and the explorer opened up a bloody trail. But quiet germs of idealism carried by the missionary and the educator followed closely in the trader's footsteps. Today the only thing

---

[1] Williams, Basil. *Cecil Rhodes.* (London, 1921.)

that keeps alive the dark man's respect for the white man is this self-same despised idealism. And the white man's day in the east is over, unless he recognizes this fact.

Victoria took over India in 1858. By the middle of the nineteenth century France had her huge colonial system in North Africa, running down into the French Congo and over into Indo-China. Portugal had acquired large African slices of territory on the eastern slopes of this vast continent. Russia penetrated into central Asia and across Siberia. Italy fought her way across North Africa into Somaliland. Germany, coming late into the field, secured southwest Africa and Tanganyika. England may be said to have dominated this whole period of expansion because her ideals and her ambitions were the centre of this new industrial revolution which had freed hands at home to go in search of new lands to conquer. It was often rivalry and jealousy of English conquests which motivated the expansion of other European powers. Moreover, in India England annexed the largest aggregation of human beings ever held in political slavery by any nation.

All of this expansion was by conquest of arms. The supposed sanction of God upon this white wave of advance apparently entitled us to trample innocent people simply because they wore no shoes and we could step on their feet. But the real justification of the white man's right to impose his civilization upon the dark man should lie in the effect which this "ordained-of-God" rule has had upon the yellow, the black, and the brown man. What has the white man done for Africa? For China? For India? Are these people any the happier, or more prosperous and contented because the white man has given them Anglo-Saxon and Latin standards?

Take Africa. Ninety-two per cent of this continent is under the control of Europe. Certainly, here the white man has had a good chance to show what he can do for the black. What has he done?

The Rand in South Africa is a big ridge which runs like a backbone across the continent, and in this backbone are the chief gold and mineral deposits which are the native wealth of Africa. For thousands of years the native black had owned the Rand. To be sure, he had never mined it, never even dreamed of the wealth which existed beneath his feet; but there can be no doubt that this gold belonged to him by right of birth. The white man came and set up his flag in South Africa and began to dig these mines. Did the black man get his share? In the oil fields of Oklahoma, the man who owns the land upon which the oil well is dug has his right to fortune as well as the operating companies who barrel and sell the oil. But in Africa the black man got a few trinkets, or nothing. The Boers began the policy which was later kept up by the British and other European powers, of confiscating any land which was discovered to have minerals, as government—white government—property. Then the government would sell it to white companies so that the profit of development would still go to white people. The black man who had owned the land got exactly nothing. What is this but organized robbery?

But certainly, we will find that the white man has at least raised the standard of living of the black man, given him a new self respect? All the white man has done for the black is to say in effect, "Here are the ideals of Christ. I do not believe them; I do not act on them. But they are great ideals. I have their symbol on the hilt of my sword!"

BLACK DIAMONDS

One of the saddest days of my life was when I visited a diamond mine at Kimberly. There were holes in the thick clay, not the shafts I had expected, and in these dirt tombs, fenced in by barbed wire entanglements and watched by armed guards, the black men were working. None could get in or out without the most degrading examination. The black workmen, as they left, were stripped naked for fear they might have secreted a diamond; rough brutal fingers pushed through their hair, stuck into their mouths, their noses, their ears. The black worker was even made to lean forward while the white guard scraped between his legs to be sure none of the black man's native wealth had stuck to him. Then, sullen and contemptuous, he was shoved through the door. Are such methods an advance in civilization for either the black man or the white? Yet the white man has dug so many diamonds out of this African clay that if he were to release them all, diamonds would be about the same price as pieces of clear glass.

On the wrist of the blacks in Rhodesia I saw the bracelet with the seal of the foreign government, showing that the black man had paid his tax to the white man and so was allowed to go from one section to another. We have put our seal upon the black man, indeed . . . but is it a sign of release to new and higher ideals of civilization, or a manacle?

We Americans have small right to criticize Europe for its treatment of the black man. Along with other white nations, we took away from him all but his very life. The stink of African slavery was only partly wiped out by the blood of our Civil War. Men are still alive in the South who were slaves.

But slavery is dead in America! says some one. Is it? Is there not such a thing as social slavery? A few weeks ago a dean of women at a negro university was run down by an automobile in a southern American city. There was a white hospital near by to which she could have been taken; but because she was black, even though she had a college degree, this woman could not enter. She was taken miles away to a negro hospital. And the doctors agreed that death came because of the delay. This is black freedom in America.

So in spite of the pious cross on his self-imposed crown, it would not seem as if the white man, anywhere in the world, except for a few individuals, has contributed very much to the black man's happiness by imposing upon him the white man's civilization.

What about the yellow man? What has the white man brought to China? Extraterritoriality. Foreign concessions. Opium. Modern business. Ideals.

FOREIGN CONCESSIONS

Extraterritoriality is a long word; a shorter word for what this means in the east is "grabbed". The real definition runs: "the state or privilege of freedom from local jurisdiction, accorded to foreign diplomatic representatives and their suites, *if prescribed by treaty;* . . . and to the citizens and subjects of Christian powers in non-Christian countries or barbarous lands, *generally by treaty.*" In other words, the white man doesn't need a treaty in non-Christian lands; he has the divine right to snatch what he wants. He has taken it for granted that

1. His civilization is superior to all others.
2. His individual rights are superior.
3. His religion is superior.
4. His right to economic profit is superior.
5. His right to go anywhere on the planet, do anything or take anything he pleases, sets all laws aside except his own.

When the white trading ships first went up the Yangtze the Chinese did not want them. They had already forbidden not only the whites but the Malays and the Indians to go up that river. But the whites refused to respect China's authority, and so sailed on. A few white people were killed. Europe leaped to arms and to battleships and demanded, in return for white blood, spilled because the traders refused to follow Chinese regulations, that China give Europe seaports where white citizens could live unmolested, could set up their own systems of government as they would in England, France, Denmark. Rivalry and jealousy over the cutting of this rich Chinese melon sprang up in Europe. If England got a free port, France wanted one, and Germany. So thoroughly was this job done, that as one historian remarks, "along the three thousand miles of Chinese coast line, there is not a single harbor in which the Chinese can freely mobilize their ships."

Not only did the Europeans demand extraterritoriality, but they began to use these bits of Europe as bases from which to commit all sorts of depredations upon China. European business men went in for banditry in a big way. Jewels, paintings, tapestries, objects of art were taken from Chinese shrines and homes, or bought for a small sum to be sold for enormous profit in the west. And just as soon as these bandits could get back to the foreign sections of these Chinese ports, they were perfectly safe. Chinese law could not touch them. Imagine having Limehouse in London or Chinatown in New York as strongholds where Chinese robbers could come back legally with booty they had snatched from American or English homes, and you will have some idea of how the system of extraterritoriality and foreign concessions has worked in China.

Naturally everyone is jealous of such exclusive rights, so that when Japan marches into Shanghai, international tension increases all over the world. Yet Japan is merely repeating what the white man has done before her, taking what she wants because she is powerful enough. No wonder the League of Nations stammers, and halts, and accomplishes very little, to date, in the way of stopping the course of Japanese conquest of this vast and rich country. We think our civilization, based upon force of arms, is superior to all others: but we want to keep it for ourselves. We feel much as the old families of a New England town regard a *nouveau riche,* when we see a yellow man breaking into our society based upon the divine right of guns.

So far the white man's civilization does not seem to be conferring such great Christian benefits upon China. True, idealists from European and American countries had been going to the Chinese, offering them Christian ideals, more hygienic methods of living. But "in the meantime and in between times" the white trader had been pressing opium upon China.

A FAMILIAR ECHO

In 1932 the Japanese is saying to the white man, "China is a drugged nation, and we are superior, and you Europeans should stand by us superior Japanese while we bring efficient government to this drugged and helpless nation." Curious irony of circumstance which permits Japan to ask the very perpetrators of China's besetting vice to allow this victim to be handed over to her! Europe does not want Japan to have China. But Europe today is in no state to fight for China: she is too financially and economically exhausted from the World War, to wish to dispute Japan's claims by modern warfare and all this entails. So the very force of arms which opened up China to foreign and economic conquest is defeating the white man in the east.

It was the East India Company which forced the sale of opium upon the Chinese. Opium was one of the greatest crops in India: the East India Company must have an enlarged market for it. China was handy. Why not teach China to smoke opium? So the white man distributed free samples of this "pipe of dreams" to arouse the Chinese appetite, and when the Chinese authorities protested against such methods, the British backed up their opium sales with guns. Armed boats from India found their way up Chinese rivers. When asked to legalize this traffic the Emperor, Tao Kwang, replied: "Nothing would induce me to receive revenue from the vice and misery of my people."

The crisis came when the Chinese commissioner at Canton burned twenty thousand cases of contraband opium. This was destroying British property! (Incidentally the East India Company was making a profit of some sixteen hundred per cent on this opium). In 1840 the British, without formal declaration of war, blockaded Canton. Does this not have an echo in today's newspaper reports? Is this not exactly what Japan is doing in China . . . trying to wash out a boycott of her goods with Chinese blood? Perhaps, if the Japanese are only persistent enough, they will get the same juicy rewards that the white man did. By the treaty of 1842 British arms had forced China to pay twenty-one million dollars indemnity, to cede the port of Hong Kong, and to open to her five other ports.

If Japan gets through with any smaller booty it may be because she has not learned her lesson from the white man well enough!

Opium could now be smuggled in through these ceded ports, and the sales mounted in China . . . and correspondingly the wretchedness of the drug addicts. The Chinese government in one last despairing effort to blot out this curse, boarded a native ship carrying contraband opium, that flew the colors of the British. To protest this disrespect for their flag, England began another bloody war in which many Chinese were killed and thirty thousand rendered homeless.

All of this happened during the last hundred years. This is no record of the period of barbarism. It was civilized Europe that thus forced opium on China. More than that it was "Christian" Europe. Sir John Bowring who wrote the hymn, "In the Cross of Christ I glory!" was the British statesman at the head of the opium trade for India. Truly the Queen should have a cross above her crown . . . but what a cross! Upon it, is a man of the east, crucified.

Is it any wonder that the prestige of the white man, founded upon force of arms, declines when the yellow man has learned to manipulate his own guns against him? When modern idealism demands an accounting of the past? But this is not all past. The British government is still selling opium in vast quantities in both China and India against organized Indian protest. And yet we wonder at the insistent cry of the new nationals, "China for the Chinese!" "Self-government for India!"

Why should not India want her freedom? What has the white man done for her but exploit her? At first the Indian did not realize that his subjugation by the British was a matter of race, of profit for the "God-elected" (self-nominated) white man, and not for the good of all.

THE ROAD TO MANDALAY

Travelling up the Irawady River I have seen more oil derricks than I have in Oklahoma. Oil is so plentiful there, that it comes out on the surface of the earth like water and the Burmans dip it up. Yet a gallon of gasoline in India costs thirty-five to sixty cents, depending on the location where you buy it. Why is this? Because the white developers of the oil of Burma have kept the price up, with tremendous profits to themselves. Most of the capital of these Burma oil wells is Scotch; the stock must be owned by white British citizens. Burmans and Indians are debarred. Here is a colossal industry which means nothing at all to the Burmese but low wages for unskilled labor. Yet the poverty of India is so great that her people pick up the dung the cows drop, for fuel. Poets have sung of the white man's burden in the east; what about the brown man's burden?

The white man has not neglected the beauty of the Burmese women. One of the most ludicrous things I ever watched was an audience of foreign missionary ladies listening to a tall lanky soloist sing them this wail:

> "On the road to Mandalay
> Where the flying fishes play,
> And the dawn comes up like thunder
> Out of China 'cross the bay!" [1]

After the ladies had applauded this great missionary hymn! the treasurer urged that a collection be taken to support the work in the land where this song was born.

A collection was needed! For one who has lived in Burma it was hard to repress a smile, at the unconscious irony of the situation. There are no flying fishes on the road to Mandalay. And the dawn in Burma could not possibly be imagined as coming up like thunder; even the dogs and cows in Burma get up lazily and languidly. Also if the dawn came up out of China it would have to rise over the mountains. But more ironical still was the fact that the money these devoted workers were giving would be used to counteract the very spirit of this rolicking white man's ditty; it would be used to protect and educate the bastard babies which the British Tommy had left upon the road to Mandalay. Not the Tommy

---

[1] Kipling, Rudyard, *Poems of Patriotism*. (New York.)

only, but commercial and other white adventurers, in oil, lumber, and rubies, who do not object to being casual parents.

From the Burmese point of view there was nothing especially wrong with the alliances the white men made with the brown women. According to Burmese law, if a man and woman have tea together or eat together, they may thereby announce their marriage. The English themselves have done much to educate and care for these children who have a drop of white blood in their veins. For two reasons. First, white prestige is thus maintained, although the child may be as black as a licorice drop. Second, the English thus obtain a buffer state of people of mixed blood, who, educated by white methods, become pathetically more imperial in mock prestige than the whites themselves. These Anglo-Indians are used by the English for the army and the police. They can trust them, because they are more foreign than the foreigners. In fact, they are native-born foreigners, imbued with the idea that all brown men are their servants.

Small wonder that Tagore has said:

"When it was day they came into my house and said,
We shall take only the smallest room here."
They said, "We shall help you in the worship of your God
And humbly accept only our share of His grace."
And they took their seat in a corner and sat there quiet and meek.
But, in the darkness of night, I find they break into my sacred shrine,
Strong and turbulent, and snatch with unholy greed
The offerings from God's altar." [1]

This is what many discerning orientals think the white man has brought to the brown, the yellow, and the black man:— robbery of his material wealth, the despoiling of his home, slavery, opium, death. Not a pleasant list for a thoughtful man

---

[1] Tagore, Rabindranath, *Gitanjali*. (New York, 1930.)

to contemplate. He hears the rumbling of the modern guns of Japan, the mutterings of a new east which has decided it can get on better without the white man. What will happen when the guns of the east grow big enough to blow to pieces those of the west? Where will the white man's policy of armed force lead him then? He has gained mountains of material wealth in the past hundred years in the Orient. He has also reaped from his sowing of force a vast, and disquieting harvest of suspicion and ill will. He has contributed to his own downfall not only by his policies in the Orient but by displaying his weakness, by leaping at his fellow white man's throat on the battlefields of Europe. The guns of the World War still echo in the east.

Japan saw in the breakdown of Europe her chance to prove her own guns the equal of the white man's. Gandhi, that is to say, India, saw in the bankruptcy of Europe the failure of armed force as a policy. Thus there has grown up in the east two contestants of the white man's power; first, Japan through force of arms; second, India through passive resistance.

Japan would never have chosen this hour to attack Shanghai had it not been for the bankruptcy of Europe. The World War which was designed to save Europe, dismembered her; displayed her weakness to the rising consciousness of power in the new Orient. The west trumped up its will to fight in France by declaring we were to achieve moral prestige, endless peace . . . a war to end war . . . but all we got out of it was a clump of white crosses. The crosses are eloquent testimony to the brown, the black, and the yellow man that the white man is not the Great White Sahib, bearing thunder in his hand, but is mortal, subject to the same bullets as the dark man.

It was another war . . . the Russo-Japanese . . . where the

yellow man gained his first intimation that by physical force he could overcome a white power. The oriental had always secretly believed himself superior to the white man in culture and background, but he had a fear complex about tackling the whites by brute strength. But when the white man, seeking new markets for his goods, forced Japan to open her doors to our western civilization, he taught the yellow man more than he bargained for; he sold him his guns along with his cast-off clothing.

During the twenty-five years since Japan defeated Russia, oriental literature, newspaper articles, and speeches have fed the east with dreams of military glory. For it is the white fields, and white meat for which the mouth of the tiger of the Orient waters. Japan says, "If we are to live sturdy lives, we must live in a temperate not a tropical climate; why not America? There is plenty of room there and the natural resources are not like Manchuria, all to be developed; here is a highly mechanized country, with its industries all ready to our hand."

COULD THIS BE TRUE?

In 1927 Tanaka, the Premier of Japan, is said to have submitted to the Emperor a memorial telling the steps he thought should be followed with reference to Manchuria. This recommendation certainly has been followed very largely in Japanese foreign policy. The same memorial says of the United States:

"The Three Eastern Provinces (Manchuria) are politically the imperfect spot in the Far East. For the sake of self protection, as well as the protection of others, Japan cannot remove the difficulties in Eastern Asia unless she adopts a policy of 'Blood and Iron'. But in carrying out this policy we have to face the United States, which has been turned against us by China's policy of fighting poison with poison. In the future, if we want to control China, we must first crush the United States just as in the past we had to fight in the Russo-Japanese war. But in order to conquer China we must first conquer Manchuria and Mongolia. In order to conquer the world, we must first conquer China. If we succeed in conquering China, the rest of the Asiatic countries and the South Sea countries will fear us and surrender to us. Then the world will realize that Eastern Asia is ours, and will not dare to violate our rights. This is the plan left to us by Emperor Meiji, the success of which is essential to our national existence."

This statement, definitely serious political document or not, is no more wild than Cecil Rhodes' dream of world empire for Britain. Its tone represents military psychology regardless of race or geography.

When the British captured Dar-es-salaam during the recent war, the Tommies upset a statue of the Kaiser that stood in the public square. The Africans laughed to see the white man with his head in the mud and his ridiculous feet in the air. But it was, nevertheless, a new idea to the black man that any white man could be made so to lose face. German or English, what difference did it make? To the black men all white men are the same; they may speak different languages . . . but does not the African himself have hundreds of dialects? That is what armed force has done to the white man in the east . . . put his head in the mud; upset his prestige.

Suppose our prestige as a white race is something worth saving. Certainly we have developed through the ages, forms and ideals worthy of perpetuation. In sheer self defense it becomes necessary for the white man to substitute for armed force a new kind of power . . . the power of organized cooperative good-will among nations. What we must build now is not a seesaw where the white man is forever up and the dark man down; but a tandem harness where both can pull their share of the world's load together.

Russia says she has this new way of cooperation. What are her four principles, as shown in the Internationale?

1. To make war impossible
2. To wipe out national boundaries
3. To transform the whole world into a cooperative commonwealth.
4. To bring about real human brotherhood and freedom.

But how is Russia going to accomplish these aims? By force. Every man, woman and child in Russia is getting military training. Yet the British Empire has tried to bring about a cooperative commonwealth and has failed only in so far as she has used force to accomplish her aims. The ideals of human brotherhood are Christian ideals: they can be attained only by Christian methods.

George Bernard Shaw who can hardly be accused of being a pious churchman has said that he did not like to believe it, but he was gradually coming to think that Jesus Christ was the best statesman the world had ever seen; that his program for individuals and nations was the only possible one. It has remained for an Indian statesman to turn these principles into a political platform, to take theoretical Christianity seriously.

"Hitherto the nations have fought in the manner of brutes," said Gandhi in his radio message to America. "They wreaked vengeance upon those they considered their enemies. We find, in searching the national anthems adopted by the great nations, that they contain imprecations upon the so-called enemies. They have vowed destruction and they have not hesitated to take the name of God and to seek divine assistance in destroying the enemy.

"We in India have endeavored to revise and reverse the process. We feel that the law governing brute creation is not the law which should guide the human race. It is inconsistent with human dignity. I, personally, would wait, if need be, for ages, rather than seek to attain the freedom of my country by bloody means.

"I feel in the innermost recesses of my heart, after a political experience extending over thirty-five years, that the world is sick unto death of blood spilling. The world is seeking a way out; and perhaps it will be the privilege of the ancient land of India to show that way."

It is curious that India rather than one of the supposedly Christian nations, should be the first to try out in practical national policy, the very ideals upon which our western civilization is based.

TOMORROW

The day of the "fighting pagan" as Gandhi calls the white warrior, is fading. His civilization based upon force in a way "unparalleled in the history of any race" is committing suicide. He came to the Orient for prestige and power. He is fast losing both because his colonial policy was based neither upon honesty nor service . . . two necessary foundations, as every modern business man knows. All indications point to the fact that sooner or later even the white man has got to come to the point where he takes into consideration every one who is human. The line beween the white and dark man can no longer be closely drawn. We each have something to give to the other, racial ideals worthy of being exchanged and rubbed smooth by the continued contact of differing minds, different peoples, into world ideals.

Gandhi's program of controlled good-will for India could easily be enlarged into a world plan. His way is probably, however, entirely too simple for European diplomats to take seriously. It is this.

First, freedom for every nation to work out its own destiny, to discover its personal and national "truth" in its own way.

Second, the granting of freedom for every one else to do the same thing. Not to take anything from any one else; not even to want it. To be satisfied with a loin cloth of homespun, if that is all you can afford for the moment.

Third, to settle disputes not by blood and guns but by economic and ethical weapons, with the power of directed public opinion.

Fourth, to be willing to sacrifice not only your property but yourself for these ideals.

That is where the hitch comes. There is sacrifice involved. Yet would it be any greater sacrifice than the world has made in France? In Belgium? There would be no bands playing; no gilt of glory; no iron crosses . . . but there would be fewer white crosses. . . .

INDEX AND GLOSSARY

Aden, 136
Afghanistan, 25
Africa, 6, 17, 30, 33, 218
Agra, vii
Ahimsa (non-violence) (harmlessness), 8, 12, 14, 16, 17, 24, 35, 56, 58, 59, 89, 129, 130
Ahmedabad, 48, 61, 126
Alien, 82
Allah (God), 190
Allahabad, 200
Ambedkar, Dr. Bhim Rao Ramji, 212
America, viii, 1, 9, 19, 24, 40, 199, 203, 229
American, 29, 80, 81
American Civil War, 48, 220
American Revolution, 69
Amritsar, 18, 20, 21, 22, 24, 25, 66
Andrews, C. F., 3, 98, 190
Anglo-Indian, 185, 227
Anglo-Saxon, viii, 95, 216, 218
Anna (two cents), 191
Anti-Asiatic Bill, 40
Arabian Sea, 187
Archbishop of Canterbury, 120
Army, 148
Arnold, Matthew, 73
Aryan, 8, 33
Ashram (community center), 48, 49, 61, 126, 137
Asia Minor, 58, 89
Asiatic Exclusion Act, 34
Asoka, 58
Australia, 18, 106

Bancroft, Frank C., 181
Bania (commercial class), 11, 30
Bayonets, 30
Bazaar (market place), 28, 158
Belgium, 55
Benares University, 209
Berlin to Bagdad Railway, 188
Bhagavad Gita, 13, 14, 77
Bible, 13, 94, 100
Bihar (Province in India), 142, 144
Bikanir, 210
Bishop, 41, 87, 98, 162, 209
Black Hole of Calcutta, 186
Black Water, 13
Boer, 6, 34, 219
Boer War, 6, 16, 60
Bolpur, 210
Bolshevik, 202
Bombay, 14, 28, 32, 52, 53, 54, 69, 169, 200
Bonfires, 158
Bose, Sir J. C., 210
Boston, 69, 81
Bowring, Sir John, 225
Boycott, 11, 62, 63, 157
Brahma, 31, 77
Brahman, 32, 75, 80, 86
Britain, 29, 82, 151
British, 17, 18, 29
British Crown, 159
British Empire, 2, 6, 40, 66, 231
British goods, 70, 176
British government, 18, 27, 65
British guns, 19
British Isles, 206
British officials, 21
British Parliament, 201
British Rule, 151, 197, 199, 210, 217
Buddha, 6, 58, 89

Buddhism, 89, 96
Buddhist, 89, 205, 206
Burka (Mohammedan woman's veil), 123
Burke, Edmund, 196
Burma, 58, 225, 226

Calcutta, vii, 1, 2, 75, 158, 170, 171
Caliph, 187
Caliphate, 186, 187
Carey, William, 101, 103, 106
Carpenter, Frederic Ives, 78
Caste, 32
Cavell, Edith, 69
Celibacy, 61
Ceylon, 58, 74
Chaplains, 163
Charka (spinning wheel), 168
Chase, Stuart, 174
Chastity, 126
Chesterton, G. K., 93, 97
Chhoti Hazri (early breakfast), 3
Child marriage, 125
China, 58, 89, 113, 198, 222, 223
Cholera, 29
Christ, 40, 56, 57, 96
Christian, 6, 40, 56, 57, 81, 85
Christian Century, 104, 105, 200, 203
Christianity, 79, 85
Churches, 79, 112
Churchill, Winston, 217
Civil Disobedience, 11, 26, 72, 77
Civilization, 2, 7, 29, 42, 94, 223, 232
Climate, 164, 165
Colleges, 83
Coolies (laborers), 28, 33, 34
Congo, 218
Conquerors, 183
Conquest, 153, 184
Continence, 43
Cotton, 156
Cow reverence, 164
Cross, 13, 56, 233
Crusades, 183
Curzon, Lord, 111

Dacca, 154, 155, 157
Dante, 53
Dar-es-salaam, 230
Declaration of Independence, 100, 196
Delhi, 111, 161, 194
Denmark, 222
Devi, Sarala, 147
Devi, Urmila, 147
Dhoti (loin cloth trousers), 64, 65
Diamonds, 219
Diplomacy, 11
Diwali (festival of lights), 110
Doctors, 210
Dominion Status, 186
Dravidians, 8
Durant, Will, 129, 185, 191
Durban, 30, 33
Durbar, 111
Dutt, R. C., 160
Dyer, General, 22, 23

East India Co., 151, 159, 160, 186, 223, 224
Ecclesiastical Department, 163
Edison, 46
Education, 177
Elwin, Verrier, 104
Emerson, 57, 77, 78, 84
England, 1, 10, 13, 78, 218
English, 9, 10, 11, 18, 24, 169
Equality, 51
Europe, 9, 16, 77, 207, 218, 223, 228
European, 11, 29, 33, 38
Exploitation, 155, 163
Extraterritoriality, 221

Famine, 116
Fanatic, 2, 6, 19, 21
Farson, Negley, 54
Fasting, 189, 190, 194
Fearlessness, 61
Ford, Henry, 2, 175, 176
Foreign Concessions, 221
Forgiveness, 25, 59
France, viii, 40, 57, 78, 203

Freedom, 5, 8, 10, 18, 62, 84, 104, 186, 197, 204, 233

Gandhiji (The Beloved), 1
Garrison, William Lloyd, 80
Germany, 40, 55, 78, 222
Ghee (clarified butter), 38
Gita, 89, 90, 91
Goat's milk, 6, 95
Golden Temple, 21

Halstead, Gordon, 103
Hartal (strike), 201
Herrick, Myron, 192
High Caste, 213
Himalayas, 64
Hindu, 13, 15, 31, 41, 79, 80, 81, 85, 87, 141, 212
Hinduism, 48, 85, 127, 128
Homespun, 233
Horniman, B. G., 22
Howe, General, 69
Humiliations, 23
Hwang, H. E., 113
Hygiene, 117, 177

Imperialism, 103, 110, 203, 216
Indentured Indians, 36, 37
Indian Opinion, 43
Indian Round Table Conference, vii
Indian Social Reformer, 80, 110, 114, 209
Industrialism, 175
Industrial workers, 66
Institutes of Manu, 92, 145, 146
Irawady River, 225
Ireland, 198
Irwin, Lord, 161, 209

Jail, 50, 51, 66, 68, 69, 137, 166
Jains, 8, 96, 110
Jallianwalla Bagh (walled garden), 22
Japan, 40, 58, 89, 107, 198, 203, 222
Japanese, 205, 223
Jazirat-ul-Arab, 187
Jesus, 6, 89, 108
Journal des Nations, 70
Justice, 20, 51

Kagawa, Toyohiko, 107
Kaiser, 216
Kaiser-i-Hind Medal, 60
Karma (cause and effect) (fate), 88, 183
Keithahn, R. R., 103
Khaddar (homespun cotton), 64, 131
Khilafat, 187
Khyber Pass, 154
Kidd, Benjamin, 133
Kimberly, 216, 219
King George V, 27
Kipling, Rudyard, 151, 226
Koran, 181, 182, 184
Korea, 58, 89

Lancashire, 132, 154, 156, 157
Landlords, 11
League of Nations, 223
Lincoln, Abraham, viii, 48, 75, 84
Lingam, 119
Liquor licenses, 28
Loin cloth, 233
London, 10, 11, 14, 32, 33, 34, 65, 77, 96, 112
Luxury, 69

MacDonald, Ramsay, 185, 191, 192
Machine age, 169, 170, 178
Machine guns, 11, 18
Madras, 75
Mahabharata, 90, 92, 127, 149
Maharajah (King), 86, 174
Mahatma (Great Soul), vii, 1
Malaria, 29
Malaviya, Pandit Madan Mohan, 209
Malays, 222
Manchuria, 229
Mandalay, 225, 226
Mantras (prayers), 134
March to the sea, 26
Marx, Karl, 5
McConnell, Bishop Francis J., 200

Mecca, 187
Mela (festival), 87, 145
Mesopotamia, 63
Meyer, F. B., 98
Miners, 66
Missionary, 79, 82, 83, 226
Missions, 100, 107, 114, 115
Mohammedans, 25, 41, 81
Money lenders, 11
Monogamy, 125
Monsoons (rainy season), 3
Montagu-Chelmsford Reforms, vii
Moplah, 190
Moral bullets, 42
Mormonism, 118
Moslem, 96, 110, 139, 158, 190
Mosque, 41
Motherland, 132
Mutiny, 56
Muzumdar, Haridas T., 16, 213

Naidu, Mrs. Sarojini, 146
Nanking, 114
Napoleon, viii, 57
Natal, 39
Natal Mercury, 38
Natarajan, K., 109, 114, 209
National Congress, 2, 4, 66, 67
Nationalism, 100, 186
Navy, 148
Negroid, 8
New Testament, 14, 85, 89, 90, 91, 182
Nizam of Hyderabad, 210
Non-violence, 8, 17, 25, 26, 59

Old Testament, 13, 43, 127
Oliver, Lord, 185
Opium, 221, 224
Orient, viii, 67, 78, 196, 228, 229, 232
Outcaste, 31, 48, 176, 211, 212

Pacifist, 26, 67
Parsees, 181
Passive resistance, 11, 20, 30, 61, 214
Passport, 103
Paton, Dr. Forester, 103
Patriots, 24
Peasants, 1, 66
Phallic worship, 118
Phillips, P. O., 162
Phoenix, Natal, 44
Picketing, 63
Plague, 29
Police, 31, 200
Politics, 75
Polygamy, 118, 121, 128, 184
Poona, 57, 144
Porbandar, 11, 15, 133, 136
Pratt, James Bissett, 184
Prestige, 217
Pretoria, 15, 33, 34
Prosperity, 35, 79
Pugari (turban) (head-gear), 146
Punjab, 20, 21, 67, 180
Purdah (the veil), 28, 122, 124

Queen Victoria, 159, 186

Rai, Lajpat, 84
Railroads, 163
Rajkot, 11, 15, 133, 136
Rebellion, 18
Red Sea, 187
Reformer, 30
Reign of terror, 23
Renaissance, 124
Retaliation, 67
Rhodes, Cecil, 216, 217, 230
Rhodesia, 219
Rifles, 22
Riots, 179, 185, 190
Roosevelt, Theodore, 75
Rothermere, Lord, 151
Round Table Conference, vii, 191, 208
Rowlatt Act, 18, 19, 67
Ruhr, 49
Russia, 45, 229, 231
Russo-Japanese war, 228

Sahib (white master), 4, 32, 186, 207, 228
Salt tax, 207
Sanskrit, 93, 108

Sarda Marriage Act, 122
Sari (woman's dress), 131
Satyagraha (soul force) (force of (truth), 16, 17, 24, 42, 43, 44, 61, 105, 140
Scholars, 69
Schools, 79
Segregation, 39
Self-determination, 5, 19, 67, 214
Self-government, 198
Sen, Mrs. P. K., 142
Sepoy Rebellion, 186
Sermon on the Mount, 12, 13, 85, 89, 95, 106
Sex, 116, 184
Sex instruction, 120
Sex worship, 119
Sha Jahan, 131
Shanghai, 222, 228
Shaw, Bernard, 16, 231
Siam, 89
Siberia, 218
Siegfried, André, 175
Sikhs, 21, 110
Slave mentality, 203, 204
Smallpox, 29
Social Workers' Congress, 148
Soldiers, 28
Somaliland, 218
South Africa, 15, 16, 35, 40, 98, 106, 219
Spinning wheel, 64, 72, 167, 168
Surgeons, 210
Swadeshi (buy Indian), 13, 61
Swaraj (Self-government), 105
Switzerland, 78

Tagore, Dr. Rabindranath, 3, 4, 24, 27, 125, 147, 210, 227
Taj Mahal, vii, 131
Tanganyika, 218
Tao Kwang, Emperor, 224
Tariff, 63, 155, 157
Tata, J. N., 209
Taxation, 27, 76, 132
Taylor, William, 106
Thoreau, Henry D., 72, 73, 84
Tibet, 58, 89
Tigris, 187
Tilak, Narayan, 52
Tolstoy, 44, 45, 71, 108, 140, 141
Transmigration, 183
Transvaal, 41, 48, 194
Truth, 57, 61, 114, 115, 233
Turkey, 187
Twain, Mark, 215

Unhappy India, 84
United States, 125, 230
Unity, 179, 188, 190
Untouchables, 79, 211, 212, 213
Usury, 165
Utah, 118

Vedas, 77, 93, 145
Versailles, Treaty of, 214
Viceroy, 1, 2, 111, 161, 204, 209
Village life, 172, 173, 211
Violence, 21, 35, 59
Vishnu Puranas, 77
Volunteers, The, 27, 28
Von Wiegand, Karl H., 200

Wall Street, 113
Washington, George, 75
White prestige, 81
Whittier, John Greenleaf, 92
Williams, Basil, 216, 217
Willingdon, Viceroy, the Earl of, 201, 204
Wilson, Woodrow, 57, 75, 84, 209
Wingfield-Stratford, Esme, 160, 197
Winslow, J. C., 52
Woolley, President Mary, 146
World War, 6, 19, 54, 228

Yangtze, 221
Yogi (ecstatic priest), 88
Youth, 4, 85, 100
Ypres, 56

Zanzibar, 136
Zenana (woman's apartment), 123
Zoroastrian, 49
Zulu, 6, 60